JOHN C. MAXWELL

LEADER SHIFT

WORKBOOK

MAKING THE ESSENTIAL CHANGES
EVERY LEADER MUST EMBRACE

TWELVE LESSONS

HarperCollins
Leadership

CONTENTS

ACKNOWLEDGMENTS

I want to say thank you to Charlie Wetzel and the rest of the team who assisted me with the formation and publication of this book. And to the people in my organizations who support it. You all add incredible value to me, which allows me to add value to others. Together, we're making a difference!

1

WHY EVERY LEADER NEEDS TO
LEADERSHIFT

Change or die.

THOMAS EDGLEY

I've been wanting to write a book on the idea of *leadershifts* for a long time because a lot has changed in the decades I've been studying and practicing leadership. In the 1970s when I was new to my career, I could find very few books on leadership. Back then, *management* ruled the business world and Peter Drucker was the king. That started to change toward the end of the 1980s, as a few authors were starting to write leadership books. People eagerly bought and read them. Why? Because they could feel that life was moving faster, change was becoming normal, and they needed a way to navigate the world's complexities, which were becoming more challenging.

People need to learn leadership to be successful. The principles of management, which had been taught for years, depended on stability and known factors. As expressed by Eric J. McNulty, director of research at the National Preparedness Leadership Initiative:

Management systems and processes tend to be linear. They assume that similar inputs will result in similar outputs. In many situations, this holds true. Leadership, however, requires a more nuanced view of the world because it involves people: what motivates them, what their interests are, and how engaged they become. Mechanical systems may be linear but as soon as the human element becomes involved the system becomes both complex and adaptive.[1]

Where management took stability for granted, leadership provides principles that work in the face of the unknown. Back in the eighties, people were looking for leaders to guide them, and people running organizations recognized the need to become leaders themselves. As they began to apply leadership principles to their world, they thrived. That's why for the last thirty years, leadership has ruled the business world.

FAST IS FASTER—FORWARD IS SHORTER

As fast as the pace was in the 1980s, when I look back it seems slow by today's standards. Life moves *much* faster now. The rate at which we must deal with change and uncertainty can seem insane.

For several years one of my organizations, the John Maxwell Team, has asked me to do short videos they post daily called Minute with Maxwell. My team will set me up in front of a camera and then give me a word or phrase, asking me to react to it or teach on it for a minute or so. It's fun and the video gets posted online as a kind of mentoring moment. Recently, for one of these sessions, the phrase they gave me was *fast forward*. What immediately came to my mind were the words *faster* and *shorter*. Here's what I mean.

The future seems to be coming at us faster than ever. It is not going to slow down. Would anybody seriously consider the idea that tomorrow will be at a slower pace than today? Technology, social media, and the rate of change will never allow that to happen. To go forward, we need to move faster. And as leaders, we need to stay ahead, we need to see more than others, and we need to see before others.

Traditionally, in athletic races, the first three finishers are recognized, and all three receive prizes. Today, outside of sports, it seems as though only winners get recognized and rewarded. As the saying goes, coming in second means you're the first loser. That's why speed and agility are so important.

Forward is also shorter. As a young leader, I was taught that to be effective in leading my organization, I should create a long-range plan of ten years, a medium-range plan of five years, and a short-range plan of two years. That seems absurd now. Today a long-range plan may be two years. Technology and innovation move so quickly that everything is going forward in a shorter time frame. As leaders, we can't drag our feet or take too long making assessments. We have to change, reread our situation, and change again. And *continue* changing.

CONSIDER

In what ways do you feel the speed of life? How does it challenge you or negatively impact you?

_____

_____

_____

_____

_____

How does a leader do more than just hang on and survive in such an environment? The key is to learn how to continually make *leadershifts*. What is a leadershift? It is an ability and willingness to make a leadership change that will positively enhance organizational and personal growth.

Educator and author Bruna Martinuzzi cited a study conducted by an organization called the Economist Intelligence Unit. It identified the top three leadership qualities that will be important in the years ahead: "the ability to motivate staff (35 percent); the ability to work well across cultures (34 percent); and the ability to facilitate change (32 percent)." All three of these qualities require adaptability. Martinuzzi likened this to the Chinese proverb that says that the wise adapt themselves to circumstances, as water molds itself to the pitcher. Perhaps at no other time in recent history has adaptability been more important than it is now. "*Adaptability*—the ability to change (or to be changed) to fit new circumstances—is a crucial skill for leaders."[2]

A more recent study conducted by Right Management and published in *The Flux Report* made it clear that the need for adaptability is only increasing. They asserted that 91 percent of future recruiting in the workplace will be based on people's ability to deal with change and uncertainty.[3]

LEADERSHIFTING IS THE ABILITY AND WILLINGNESS TO MAKE A LEADERSHIP CHANGE THAT WILL POSITIVELY ENHANCE ORGANIZATIONAL AND PERSONAL GROWTH.

Good leaders adapt. They shift. They don't remain static because they know the world around them does not remain static. This has always been true, but it's never been more obvious than today, nor has the ability to change quickly been more important. Adaptable leaders who make leadershifts lean into uncertainty and deal with it head on. I like what Paul Karofsky, executive director emeritus of Northeastern University's Center for Family Business, said about this, though he used the word *ambiguity* instead of *uncertainty*:

Ambiguity may keep people up nights, but anyone seeking exquisite simplicity in his or her career ought to look for a non-leadership position.

Leaders, by definition, have followers. Followers need direction. Direction requires decision-making. Decision-making requires consideration of options. And consideration of options involves dealing with uncertainty.[4]

If you want to be successful as a leader, you need to learn to become comfortable with uncertainty and make shifts continually. You need to be flexible and deal with uncertainty without losing focus. Leaders who leadershift must be like water. They have to be fluid. Water finds a way, then makes a way. First it changes with its circumstances. The environment dictates the change. But moving water is also forceful. It first moves around an object, but at the same time it begins moving the object. It can wear down solid rock over time. A seemingly small shift can make a big difference. Simple and obvious it may be. Trivial it is not.

ASSESS

On a scale of one (poor) to ten (fantastic), how comfortable are you with uncertainty normally?

1   2   3   4   5   6   7   8   9   10

On a scale of one (poor) to ten (fantastic), how flexible are you naturally?

1   2   3   4   5   6   7   8   9   10

On a scale of one (poor) to ten (fantastic), how well are you able to remain focused when facing uncertainty?

1   2   3   4   5   6   7   8   9   10

On a scale of one (poor) to ten (fantastic), how confident are you while changing and dealing with uncertainty?

1   2   3   4   5   6   7   8   9   10

CONSIDER

How do you think these characteristics will impact your ability to leadershift?

_____

_____

_____

_____

_____

_____

_____

The truth is this: *every advance you make as a leader will require a leadershift that changes the way you think, act, and lead.* If you want to be an effective leader, you must leadershift. You cannot be the same, think the same, and act the same if you hope to be successful in a world that does not remain the same.

As Malcolm Gladwell said, "That's your responsibility as a person, as a human being—to constantly be updating your positions on as many things as possible. And if you don't contradict yourself on a regular basis, then you're not *thinking*."[5]

YOU CANNOT BE THE SAME, THINK THE SAME, AND ACT THE SAME IF YOU HOPE TO BE SUCCESSFUL IN A WORLD THAT DOES NOT REMAIN THE SAME.

Leadershifting moves us forward in the face of the natural temptation to be mentally rigid. It prompts us to become more innovative and get out of our comfort zones, question conventional wisdom, and welcome change. Every leadershift you make has the potential to make you a better leader.

ARE YOU READY TO SHIFT AS A LEADER?

Before I talk about the practices involved in leadershifting, I want to lay the groundwork by describing the mind-set needed to leadershift.

ASSESS

YES NO
❑   ❑   Are you ready to change?
❑   ❑   Are you willing to start asking more questions instead of giving more answers?

❑   ❑   Are you willing to become a better listener?

❑   ❑   Are you willing to become a better observer?

❑   ❑   Are you willing to rely more on your intuition and your creativity?

If you answered no to any of these questions, you are resisting change and will need to adopt a new mindset in order to leadershift.

Leadershifting will require you to rely on values, principles, and strategy, but it will also push you to rely on innovation, to seek out options, to harness creativity. You'll also need to let go of some things and be dedicated to getting better.

Leadershifting is not easy, especially when you first start doing it. Often you leave behind something that has worked to pursue something untested. You'll have to deal with the tension between the stability that gives security and the adaptability that opens up opportunity. That will empower you to get better, to become someone new before you can grow into something new. The desire to improve will drive you to keep learning. But here's the good news: learning to leadershift will make you a better leader!

YOU'LL HAVE TO DEAL WITH THE TENSION BETWEEN THE STABILITY THAT GIVES SECURITY AND THE ADAPTABILITY THAT OPENS UP OPPORTUNITY.

HOW TO LEADERSHIFT

As we move forward in this book, I'll take you through eleven major leadershifts I've made in my leadership journey. But before we do that, I want to teach you seven things you must do to leadershift successfully. Embrace these practices daily, and you will be ready to face every leadershift situation with flexibility and confidence.

1. CONTINUALLY LEARN, UNLEARN, AND RELEARN

I've already discussed the pace at which our world is changing. I recently read an article published by the World Economic Forum that brought light to this.

> To quote Harvard Business Review's "Mind the (Skills) Gap": "The lessons learned in school can become outdated before student loans are paid off." As it points out, the skills college graduates acquire during a bachelor's degree that used to provide enough basic training to last a career, today have an expected shelf life of only five years. . . . Or, as lynda.com author Mark Niemann-Ross states bluntly: "In four years, you'll have to relearn 30% of your job."[6]

How are leaders to thrive in this environment? We must learn, unlearn, and relearn. This process is essential for leadershifting. We have to embrace change every day. We must be willing to let go of what worked yesterday and learn new ways of seeing, doing, and leading. We cannot afford to be in love with any one technology or methodology. We keep learning and changing, or our leadership dies.

2. VALUE YESTERDAY BUT LIVE IN TODAY

Baseball great Babe Ruth is rumored to have said, "Yesterday's homerun doesn't win today's game." Isn't that fantastic? It's a good reminder for us to focus on today. What we did in the past may look good on a resume, but it won't help us win today.

For years I had a sign in my office that said, "Yesterday Ended Last Night." I put it there to remind me that all the good I did yesterday won't guarantee a good day for me today, nor will all the bad that happened yesterday mean that today has to be bad. Today stands on its own. If I want a great today, I need to do what's necessary now. I can and should be grateful for yesterday, but I have to focus on today.

3. RELY ON SPEED, BUT THRIVE ON TIMING

Having to move quickly in today's climate isn't really a choice if you want to succeed. However, timing is. As a leader who leadershifts, you need to understand the context of your environment. What is happening around you determines whether you hold fast or move forward. Leading is like knowing when to eat a pear. It's said that there is only one day in the life of a pear when it is perfect to eat. As a leader you must be able to recognize the right timing of leadershift moments. When does a team member need an encouraging pep talk and when do they need to be challenged to step up? When is the right time to add a new product or to retire an existing one that has already seen its best days? When should your organization use some of its cash to seize an opportunity, and when is that a bad idea? For leaders, timing is critical.

4. See the Big Picture as the Picture Keeps Getting Bigger

My journey leading people really began when I first understood that everything rises and falls on leadership. This truth became the foundation upon which I built my life. It continues to be the catalyst for my personal development and my training of others.

When people started asking me to speak on leadership, I didn't have much to teach. Later when I decided to write a book on the subject, I thought it would be my only one. Now I've been leading people and training leaders for more than forty-five years, and my perspective has been enlarged tremendously. The more I learn about the subject, the more I recognize I don't know enough about it. The more leadership experiences I gain, the more I realize I would benefit from more experience. There is no finish line when it comes to improving, and there is no complete picture of leadership that can be mastered. As long as I'm growing, my leadership picture will continue to enlarge. If you keep growing, yours will too.

I like to think of this process as layered learning. Each time we learn a new lesson and connect it with the many things we've already learned on the same subject, we gain depth and we see more of the big picture. This process requires time; no one can learn all the lessons at once. Putting together lessons requires intentionality, but when you do, you expand your knowledge.

5. Live in Today but Think About Tomorrow

Leaders have a natural bias toward action. They have to be proactive today for the sake of tomorrow. However, the longevity of their leadership is determined by how they think and see the future. Staying ahead of the team comes from thinking ahead of the team. If you think ahead, you can stay ahead. As political columnist George Will said, "The future has a way of arriving unannounced." We cannot recover yesterday, but tomorrow is ours to win or lose.

How can we do that as leaders? What can we do today to ensure we have what we need to lead tomorrow? We have to practice what I call advance attraction, which I discovered in the 1980s. I concluded that I could experience a positive future only if I had a good dream and a good team. At that time, my dream excited me, but my team did not. How was I going to attract the team I needed to fulfill my dream?

The first step toward getting a better team for the future was to know what I wanted and needed. I started by writing down the qualities of the team I wanted to have. This developed an increased awareness in me that promoted advance attraction. Here's how this works.

> When you know who you are and you know what you want, you then
> know the kind of people you will attract, and the things you will discover.
>> Your mind will think things that will help you get what you want.
>> Your eyes will see things that will help you get what you want.
>> Your heart will feel things that will help you get what you want.
>> Your attitude will believe things that will help you get what you want.
>> Your mouth will say things that will help you get what you want.
>> Your actions will attract things that will help you get what you want.

As I attracted and discovered the kinds of team members I needed to realize my dream, I began to experience positive results. Today I'm abundantly reaping the benefits of this leadershift.

6. Move Forward Courageously in the Midst of Uncertainty

Life expands or shrinks in proportion to our courage. When leaders fail to make a necessary leadershift because of fear or uncertainty, it only increases their fear, which results in frustration. The greater the inaction of the leaders, the more opportunities they lose because opportunities are always surrounded by uncertainty. All good things include uncertainty, and overcoming uncertainty requires courage.

I like what Brad Lomenick said about courage in his book *The Catalyst Leader*. He quoted my friend Andy Stanley, a wonderful leader who founded North Point Church. Andy was speaking to Catalyst leaders, but his words also described leaders who leadershift:

Many, many great things have begun with a single act of courage, throughout history and today. A person steps out and makes one courageous decision and that one domino starts many other dominoes falling. We have to step out and take that first step, and we may never know the ripple effect of that one courageous decision. Catalyst leaders—your decision to do something courageous may result in something greater than you ever imagined. Step out. . . .

Fear in leadership usually is connected to the uncertainty about the future. But uncertainty about the future is never going to go away. I tell leaders all the time—uncertainty is why there are leaders. Uncertainty gives you job security. Wherever there is uncertainty, there will always be a need for leaders, which means always stepping out into the unknown, always requiring courage.[7]

Betty Bender, former president of the Library Administration and Management Association, said, "Anything I've ever done that ultimately was worthwhile initially scared me to death." When faced with uncertainty, as leaders we need to move forward courageously.

7. Realize Today's Best Will Not Meet Tomorrow's Challenges

If you want to become good at leadershifting, you need to keep getting better, because tomorrow's challenges will not be won with today's abilities. Here's my strategy for getting better. My goal at the end of each day is to feel satisfied because I gave my very best, but my goal at the beginning of each day is to be dissatisfied enough to try to improve on yesterday. This interplay of dissatisfaction and satisfaction creates a tension that makes me want to improve.

As I approach a new day, I try to be my best. That will make tomorrow better. The best way to have good choices tomorrow is to make the right choices today. The best way to realize the changes we want tomorrow is to make the needed changes today. The best way to meet the challenges of tomorrow is to do our best in the challenges of today. I can't skip today and hope tomorrow is better. So every day I ask myself, "Is this the best I can do today?" In this way, I'm following the advice of my hero and mentor John Wooden, who said to make today your masterpiece.

At the same time, I don't rest on my best. You've heard that good is the enemy of great, but best is the enemy of better. I have to cultivate the dissatisfaction required to get better. I purposely create that tension every day. The question, "Is this the best I can do today?" helps me to make the most of today. The question, "Am I getting better?" spurs me on to change. I want to grow into tomorrow's challenges, not just go into them. If I keep getting better, I can leadershift better tomorrow. Yesterday's best is the foundation for tomorrow's improvement.

ASSESS

If you want to keep getting better so that you can become a better leadershifter, then

- *Learn something new:* Ask yourself, "When's the last time I learned something for the first time?"

    Your answer: _____

- *Try something different:* Ask yourself, "When's the last time I did something for the first time?"

    Your answer: _____

- *Find something better:* Ask yourself, "When's the last time I found something better for the first time?"

    Your answer: _____

- *See something bigger:* Ask yourself, "When's the last time I saw something bigger for the first time?"

    Your answer: _____

Keep in mind: everyone can improve, and everything can be improved. Every day has improvement possibilities. Now you understand the framework for leadershifting:

- Continually Learn, Unlearn, and Relearn
- Value Yesterday but Live in Today
- Rely on Speed but Thrive on Timing
- See the Big Picture as the Picture Keeps Getting Bigger
- Live in Today but Think About Tomorrow
- Move Forward Courageously in the Midst of Uncertainty
- Realize Today's Best Will Not Meet Tomorrow's Challenges

COMMIT

Are you willing to commit yourself to becoming someone who leadershifts? If so, sign your name to this commitment statement:

I commit myself to this process. The first leadershift I will make is in the way that I think about leadership. I will continually learn, unlearn, and relearn. I will value yesterday but live in today. I will rely on speed but thrive on timing. I will strive to see the big picture even as the picture keeps changing and getting bigger. I will live in today but think about tomorrow. And I will move forward courageously in the midst of uncertainty. I will continually make leadership changes that will positively enhance both organizational and personal growth.

_____   _____
Signature   Date

The rest of this book focuses on the most important leadershifts I have made over the years. Without a doubt, these shifts have strengthened and sustained my leadership. Each has changed my course, setting me in a new and better direction. Each has allowed me to gain new leadership territory and grow inwardly. Each has shed light on my leadership journey, and I believe they will help yours. Even a small shift can make a big difference.

However, these are *examples* of leadershifting, not a blueprint. The leadershifts you need to make will be unique to your journey. While it's true that some of yours may be similar to mine, many will not be. But don't forget: *every advance you make as a leader will require a leadershift that changes the way you think, act, and lead.* When you make a leadershift, it will make you a better leader.

As you go through this workbook, you will need to continually shift from action to reflection. I will ask questions and present challenges so that your best leader can emerge. The leadershifts in this workbook will not take you from bad to good. They will take you from good to better. If you try to make some small shift in that direction every day, you can and will reach your leadership potential.

WHY EVERY LEADER NEEDS TO
LEADERSHIFT

DISCUSSION QUESTIONS

1. What causes you the greatest frustration when it comes to the need for speed and innovation in the workplace? Why?

2. Do you tend to be a proactive catalyst for change or a reactive adapter to change? How does this impact your leadership?

3. Which of the seven daily practices listed below do you think will be easiest for you to adopt? How will it help you?

   - Continually Learn, Unlearn, and Relearn
   - Value Yesterday but Live in Today
   - Rely on Speed but Thrive on Timing
   - See the Big Picture as the Picture Keeps Getting Bigger
   - Live in Today but Think About Tomorrow
   - Move Forward Courageously in the Midst of Uncertainty
   - Realize Today's Best Will Not Meet Tomorrow's Challenges

4. Which of the seven will be the most difficult to adopt? Why?

5. In what area of your current leadership are you sensing a need to make a leadershift? Why do you believe you need to make a change? How are you hoping change will help you?

NOTES

LESSON TWO

SOLOIST TO
CONDUCTOR

THE FOCUS SHIFT

One is too small a number to achieve greatness.

THE LAW OF SIGNIFICANCE

One of the first and most important shifts anyone must make to become a leader is from soloist to conductor. You can be a successful person on your own, but not a successful leader. I began to learn this lesson and make this shift in 1974 when I heard Zig Ziglar for the first time. Zig, who later became a good friend, made a positive impact on millions of lives, and mine was one of them.

That first time I went to see him speak, I was mesmerized. He was so dynamic. I had been trained to speak and had been speaking for about five years, but Zig was different. He moved back and forth on the stage. His delivery was distinctive with his Southern drawl. He paced his words for impact. He had charm. At one point, he even knelt to make a point and connect with us.

I loved everything about what he did that day, but what made the greatest impression on me was a statement he made. It became the catalyst for taking my leadership mind-set from soloist to conductor. Zig said, "You can get everything in life you want if you will just help enough other people get what they want."

Those words struck me like a bolt of lightning. Immediately I realized that my leadership focus was wrong. I was like a soloist who wanted the entire orchestra to serve me and my agenda. Instead, I needed to act like a conductor who worked to bring out the best in everyone around me. My agenda needed to change to how I could help others, not just myself.

Over the next couple of years, my focus shifted from me to we and I made a discovery. My increased effort to first focus on others and add value to them increased the energy of those I led—and it increased my energy while I was leading them. That's when I discovered that it's wonderful when the people help their leader, but it's even more wonderful when the leader helps the people.

> **MY INCREASED EFFORT TO FIRST FOCUS ON OTHERS AND ADD VALUE TO THEM INCREASED THE ENERGY OF THOSE I LED— AND IT INCREASED MY ENERGY WHILE I WAS LEADING THEM.**

Recently I read an article about four musical soloists who have transitioned to become conductors. South Korean Han-Na Chang, who has enjoyed a successful international career as a cellist, recently became a full-time conductor. When asked why she began conducting, she replied:

> I am drawn to the great symphonic and operatic literature, and also by the music-making and collaboration that exists between the conductor and the orchestra. . . . Collaborating with the orchestra is tremendously rewarding: Every orchestra is different, so the conductor is always trying to find the most effective way of conducting that particular orchestra, in order to unite the group behind a common vision and interpretation.[1]

Chang pointed out that conducting is completely different from being a soloist. "When I play my instrument," she said, "what I think quite naturally and instantaneously translates into sound; when conducting, I'm making sound with a group of individuals. The possibilities and the potential of the sound of an orchestra are virtually limitless, and this is truly fascinating to me."

CHALLENGES LEADERSHIFTING FROM SOLOIST TO CONDUCTOR

The potential of a group is always greater than that of an individual. People working together possess limitless possibilities. They can work together to do something greater than themselves. And when they bond, they enjoy the journey of working even more. However, that doesn't mean that working together doesn't have its own challenges. When you transition from soloist to conductor, there are some realities you have to face:

1. GOING SLOWER SO YOU CAN GO FARTHER

You've probably heard the old expression "it's lonely at the top" applied to leadership. But think about that statement. If you're at the top all alone, where are the people you're supposed to be leading? Shouldn't they be at the top with you? If you're at the top alone, it means you took off ahead of your people and left them behind. If you climb the peaks of success alone, you're not a leader. You're a hiker. You're a leader only if you have your people with you. Your pace will be slower, but you will journey together.

Good leaders don't go to the top alone and then yell down, "Hey, people, come on up—if you can figure out how to make the climb." They make a conscious decision to slow down. They carefully choose their steps so that they can help others make the climb with them.

Think about how this must have been for cellist Han-Na Chang when she shifted from soloist to conductor. As a musician she could pick up her instrument anytime she wanted, play any music she wanted, and do so however long she wanted. She could focus on any part of the music desired or on any aspect of her technique, with no regard for others. Now, as a conductor, she can't do that. She has to make arrangements. She has to be on other people's schedules. She has to take into consideration the abilities and personalities of a large group of people. She has to communicate her vision. And in the end, she bears responsibility for their success or failure.

As I've already mentioned, leaders have a natural bias for action. Good leaders see more than others do, and they see before others do. It's in their DNA to move quickly and decisively. So their natural inclination is often to run fast on their own, to climb as high as they can. But to lead others successfully, leaders need to travel with their people, not run or climb ahead of them.

2. RECOGNIZING THAT YOU NEED OTHERS

Another reality you must recognize when transitioning from soloist to conductor is your need for other people. You can't produce the music of an orchestra when you're trying to be a one-man (or one-woman) band. Before I heard Zig Ziglar speak and realized I needed to make a leadershift, I only thought of how people needed me. I believed I was the key to their success. But after I started focusing on helping others, I began to understand how much I needed them. Only by working together and helping one another would we be able to become successful.

Once I made that discovery, I began creating an environment where people worked together to add to one another's strengths and offset one another's weaknesses. I asked others to come alongside me and make up for my leadership deficits. I, in turn, worked to apply my strengths to their weaker areas. I made it my goal to cultivate an environment where we put completing one another ahead of competing with one another.

CONSIDER

Look at the difference between the two attitudes and mark the one on each line that most often describes you:

COMPETING
- ❑ Has a Scarcity Mind-set
- ❑ Thinks Win-Lose
- ❑ Practices Single Thinking
- ❑ Excludes Others

COMPLETING
- ❑ Has an Abundance Mind-set
- ❑ Thinks Win-Win
- ❑ Practices Shared Thinking
- ❑ Includes Others

A completing culture creates wins for everyone. It lifts morale. It encourages team members to make one another better. People enjoy working in such an environment.

As I worked to create a culture and environment where completing was valued, I better understood how I needed others. I also began enjoying what we were doing together.

3. Making the Effort to Understand Others

Many entrepreneurs and high achievers are able to work alone. Like good soloist musicians who choose to play in the subway, they can create music without the assistance of any other musicians. It's also true that some soloists are so talented that others are willing to work with them, even if the soloist is egotistical and inconsiderate. But no one can become a good conductor without making the effort to understand other people.

I have to confess, in my early years of leadership, I didn't give enough attention to the people I was leading. As a soloist leader, I thought the symphony was there simply to accompany me. I only wanted people to understand and embrace my vision, my agenda, my journey, my talents, my heart. To make the leadershift from soloist to conductor, I had to consider everyone else. I needed to understand and embrace their thoughts, desires, talents, contribution, and journey.

Several years ago I was speaking in Buenos Aires, Argentina. One evening my host took me to a large ballroom where we watched a huge exhibition of people dancing the tango. There must have been two hundred people out on the floor in beautiful costumes. They were fantastic. Their sense of movement and rhythm was wonderful. I greatly enjoyed watching them.

Years before, my wife, Margaret, and I had taken ballroom dance lessons, so I had a little bit of appreciation for how difficult dancing is. The tango looked very complicated and difficult to execute with precision. I knew that my host was an excellent dancer, so I asked him, "What enables them to dance so flawlessly and effortlessly?"

He said that the key was understanding your partner's point of view. "To be able to lead properly," he said, "you want to understand how it feels to be led. In the tango, you cannot lead without having the sense of the follower." That made sense to me. The follower has to be able to trust the leader, and she must be able to move with him in time with the music. Only together can they accomplish the dance. That cooperation and understanding also applies equally to good leadership.

4. Wanting Others to Shine More Than You Do

My host in Argentina also shared another insight about the tango that applies to leaders who shift from soloist to conductor. He explained that the dancer who leads sets up the dancer who follows for success. The leader provides the foundation and makes it possible for both of them to successfully execute the intricate serpentine steps and kicks. As a result, the follower gives the tango its full expression. The more secure and solid the leader is, the more the follower is able to shine.

Good leaders who conduct rather than go solo want the people who work with them to shine. Every day I look for opportunities to lift up people. To do it, I follow a simple formula:

- see the possibilities in all people,
- honor them in front of others,
- invite them to help achieve the vision,
- notice what they do well and compliment them, and
- thank them to make sure they know they're valued.

None of these actions takes brilliance or a high degree of skill. But they do all require intentionality. If you want to become a good conductor, give them a try. Help others to shine.

5. Helping Others to Become Better Every Day

To become a successful leadership conductor, you must go slower so you can go further, recognize that you need others, make the effort to understand others, and want others to shine more than you do. But you will also need to learn how to do things every day that help the people you lead to improve. This requires taking the focus off yourself and looking for ways you can help others reach their potential. Sometimes that can be a challenge.

A few years ago, I was getting ready to speak to a large group in Kiev, Ukraine, and my interpreter and I were in the green room getting acquainted. We had never worked together, but as we chatted, it became clear that he was familiar with me because he had read a lot of my books.

About ten minutes before I was scheduled to go out onstage, I could tell he was wanting to communicate something important to me. He said, "I know you teach a lot about leaders adding value to others, but you need to know that message will not work here. For three generations, people here have been under leadership that has taken value from them, not added value to them."

As he left to prepare for our time onstage, I sat in my chair and realized that I had a big challenge ahead of me. How could I expect the people to help others when the only model of leadership they'd ever seen had leaders who took from them and added value only to themselves? How could I connect with them?

That night I walked out onstage and asked, "How many of you are suspicious of leaders?" It looked like every hand was raised.

"How many of you have been hurt by leaders?" Once again, hands were raised everywhere. Then I said to the audience, "Everything rises and falls on leadership. For three generations, you have experienced leadership that makes everything fall. Tonight I'm going to help you learn how to help people, add value to them, and help them rise under your leadership."

I went on to give them the three questions followers ask of their leaders:

1. Do you care for me?
2. Can I trust you?
3. Can you help me?

As I said each question, I asked if it resonated with them, and each time they affirmed that it did. Making the shift so that you're doing something every day to add value to others makes good leadership possible.

REFLECT

How would the people you lead respond to these three questions? Would they say they *know* you care for them? Would they say they *know* they can trust you?

(continued)

Would they say they *know* you can help them and want to? What evidence do you have that they believe you are entirely trustworthy as a leader?

_____

_____

_____

_____

CHANGE YOUR FOCUS FROM RECEIVING TO GIVING

As I've already mentioned, as a young leader I was focused on how people could help me, not on how I could help them and add value to them. My thinking was selfish. It was also shortsighted. Having lived in a farming community early in my career, I should have known better. I should have thought about the sowing and reaping principle: sowing always precedes reaping.

As leaders, our question each day should not be, "Will I reap a harvest?" Instead, it should be, "Have I sowed seeds today?" I know—I'm changing my metaphor from music to farming, but stay with me. Said another way, am I trying to add value or take value? Am I focused on receiving or giving? As a soloist, it's very easy to make everything about myself: How am I performing? Is the orchestra making me sound good? Is my technique as good as I want it to be? Is my audience appreciating me and my performance? Is this moment helping my career?

Good leaders shift from being self-focused to others-focused. They give more than they take. They focus on sowing not reaping. As leaders, we need to maintain a seed-sowing mind-set. What does that mean? It means we should . . .

- Focus on adding value daily.
- Add as much value as possible as often as possible.
- Never wait to add value.
- Give without keeping score so motives stay pure.
- Welcome any return as an unexpected blessing.

I want to spend the remainder of this Lesson on the idea of adding value to those we "conduct." I want to drill down on each aspect of this mind-set so that you can embrace and practice it as a leader. So let's tackle each one in turn:

1. Focus on Adding Value Daily

Every day I look at my calendar and ask myself, *Where can I add value today?* This question prepares me mentally to be ready to add value to others within the framework of my day. I review the scheduled meetings and activities to discover where I can be intentional about helping people.

I also ask myself, *What additional opportunities to help others will be given to me today?* When I ask myself this question in the morning, I usually don't know what the answer will be. But by asking it, I create positive anticipation, which prepares me mentally and emotionally to seek out and identify moments when I will be able to sow positive seeds in the lives of others.

My experience over the years has convinced me that we receive what we believe, and that applies to opportunities to add value to others. Because I expect to have many opportunities, I'm able to act on them.

CONSIDER

What are you normally focused on as you begin your day? Is it on adding value and sowing seeds? Or is it on receiving value and reaping a harvest? How does this impact the opportunities you receive?

_____

_____

_____

_____

_____

2. Add As Much Value As Possible As Often As Possible

It's clear that there is a direct relationship between the seeds we sow and the harvest we reap. The amount of value we add to others determines the possible return. The fewer the seeds, the smaller the harvest. The more the seeds, the greater the harvest. This seems obvious. So, I have a question for you. Why do so many people sow so few seeds? Why do people not give more generously to others? Why do people not help others more? Everyone would like to reap a great harvest. I would, wouldn't you? How can you hope to have a big return with a small investment? The foundation and core of every realized dream come from sowing positive seeds. As leaders, we must stop wishing and start working. Instead of looking for the "secret sauce" of success, we must start sowing seeds of success.

AS LEADERS, WE MUST STOP WISHING AND START WORKING. INSTEAD OF LOOKING FOR THE "SECRET SAUCE" OF SUCCESS, WE MUST START SOWING SEEDS OF SUCCESS.

CONSIDER

What is preventing you from being more generous with your time and resources? What can you do immediately to change that?

_____

_____

_____

_____

_____

_____

3. NEVER WAIT TO ADD VALUE

Too many people wait to do good. It's as though they're waiting for permission. Or inspiration. But we should never delay sowing seeds that benefit others. Instead, we should follow the motto: be the first to give or add value to another person when you can.

When you add value to others—especially when you do it early and unprompted—you inspire others with your example. I know I've been inspired by the positive actions of others. For example, when my mentor Les Parrott shared with me that the reason he wrote books was to add value to people, I was inspired to start doing the same. Going back to my childhood, when I watched my father walk slowly through the crowd to touch the lives of others, I could see how people positively responded to him, and I wanted to do the same. These examples inspired me to be more giving, to sow seeds into the lives of others.

Don't hesitate to help another person by sowing a positive seed in his or her life. Add value as early and often as you can. Help others to "play music better." You just might become the leader someone remembers for encouraging them to greatness.

CONSIDER

What most often keeps you adding value to others? What small change can you make to speed up your giving?

_____

_____

_____

_____

_____

4. GIVE WITHOUT KEEPING SCORE SO MOTIVES STAY PURE

I know that I've already explained how we can't reap a harvest if we don't sow seeds, and we can't get a return without first giving. But receiving should not be our motive for giving. We live in a tit-for-tat culture. People are willing to scratch our backs if we're willing to scratch theirs. As leaders who add value to others, we should never keep score. We should sow seeds because it's the right thing to do. That's the only way to be sure our motives remain pure.

My thinking has changed over the years in this area. In the beginning, I was motivated by the return I would receive. I was focused on the harvest. I already shared how Zig Ziglar's quote about helping others changed my focus. But over time, I realized that placing emphasis on the return was diminishing the joy of helping others. I was thinking about how much and how long I had to give, not on how I was helping. Besides, when you add value to others, there isn't a guaranteed return.

My attitude began shifting when I remembered the words of Jesus, who said: "Whenever you did one of these things to someone overlooked or ignored, that was me—you did it to me."[2] Because I'm a person of faith, those words convicted me. But they also assured me. God sees the value we add to others, and it's like we did it for him. That finally brought me to the correct belief about helping others—that it is the right thing to do. It's always the right thing to do—anytime, anyplace, anyone. And the right way to do it is any way you can. Any day we are giving is a good day—and we should never keep score.

5. WELCOME ANY RETURN AS AN UNEXPECTED BLESSING

When my leadership mind-set began focusing on adding value by sowing positive seeds in the lives of others, I became more creative about how I could do that. I started my career by speaking once a week to my tiny congregation. Soon I started creating resources and sharing them. In time, I added writing. I started teaching at conferences, and later I started hosting my own events. I trained leaders so that they could train the people who followed them. Beginning in 2009, I expanded to include social media. I started companies that develop leaders in businesses and corporations. And I started training coaches.

All that time, my focus was on adding value. My goal was only to sow seeds, but I have to say, the return has been incredible. The influence I have been given and the value I've added is far greater than I ever imagined it could be. And it feels as though the harvest has multiplied way beyond the seeds I've sown. That has been a great blessing. If you keep sowing seeds and you do it while focused on the giving rather than the receiving, I believe you, too, will receive a harvest of unexpected blessings.

* * *

These are my thoughts on adding value. And that's what leaders do who shift from soloist to conductor. They focus on helping others to be their best. In the end, can you be a successful person as a soloist? The answer is undoubtedly yes. Can you be a successful leader? I would say maybe, but only in a very limited way. To reach your leadership potential—and more importantly, to help others reach their individual and team potential—you need to make the shift from soloist to conductor. If you are willing to make that shift and do the work of leading others well, then you might have the opportunity to live a life like the one described by author Matthew Kelly, who wrote:

> In a land where there are no musicians;
> > In a land where there are no storytellers, teachers, and poets;
> > In a land where there are no men and women of vision and leadership;
> > In a land where there are no legends, saints, and champions;
> In a land where there are no dreamers,
> > The people will most certainly perish.
> > But you and I, we are the music makers;
> > We are the storytellers, teachers, and poets;
> > We are the men and women of vision and leadership;
> > We are the legends, the saints, and the champions;
> > And we are the dreamers of the dreams.[3]

I would add that we are the conductors, who help others make beautiful music together.

TAKE ACTION

Become a positive conductor in the lives of others. Every day this week, focus on giving rather than receiving from others. Do that by creating a plan to add value:

- *Focus on Adding Value Daily* — What do you have that you can offer to others?

_____

_____

_____

_____

- *Add as Much Value as Possible as Often as Possible*—How will you use it to add value?

  _____
  _____
  _____
  _____

- *Never Wait to Add Value*—When will you use it?

  _____
  _____
  _____
  _____

- *Give Without Keeping Score*—How can you give generously with no thought of return?

  _____
  _____
  _____
  _____

SOLOIST TO
CONDUCTOR

THE FOCUS SHIFT

DISCUSSION QUESTIONS

1. Do you naturally think like a soloist or a conductor? What examples can you give to illustrate?

2. What do you find most rewarding about working alone? What do you find the most challenging? Why?

3. What do you find the most rewarding about working with others? What do you find the most challenging? Why?

4. In addition to adding value to others, what other actions and attitudes actively promote cooperation and collaboration among people working together?

5. What is the single greatest change you need to make in order to make the leadershift to conductor? What will you do immediately to facilitate it?

NOTES

LESSON THREE

GOALS TO
GROWTH

THE PERSONAL DEVELOPMENT SHIFT

Improving yourself is the first step in improving everything else.

UNKNOWN

When I started my leadership career, I had two goals. I wanted to help the people in my congregation, and I hoped to someday—by the end of my career—grow a church to an attendance of five hundred people. I had a pretty good sense of how to accomplish the first task. I had watched my father help people every day of my life, plus I had natural people skills. But I had no idea how to go about accomplishing the second task other than to work hard.

In *The 15 Invaluable Laws of Growth*, I wrote about a meeting I had in 1972 with Curt Kampmeier, a salesman from Success Motivation. Curt introduced me to a personal growth kit that cost a whopping $799. It took Margaret and me six months to scrape together the money, and I bought the kit.

I look back now at what that kit taught, and it was really simple: the basics of goal-setting and follow-through. But it was significant to me because it helped me to create a track to run on for identifying goals, breaking them down into manage-able steps, and following through with the disciplines to get them done. I spent three years working from that growth kit, and hitting goals became a consistent part of my professional life.

During that period, I read an article about the fastest-growing churches in the country, and I got excited. *What if we could make our church one of them? What if we could become the fastest-growing church in the state of Ohio,* I thought. That became my goal. It was a big goal, a huge goal for me. The church was already close to my lifetime goal of five hundred people, and I was only in my twenties. But I was willing to strive for it. I won't bore you with all the details, but we succeeded in doubling the size of the congregation in one year, and in 1975 we were recognized as the fastest-growing church in Ohio. And we all celebrated.

When you hit a goal like that, once the celebration is done, you start asking yourself the question, *What's next?* And that's what I started to do. I wondered what I should try to do next. Did I want to attempt the same thing next year? Was there a different goal I should be going after?

As I reflected and explored ideas, I came to a realization. The lessons I'd learned while working to grow the church were actually more important—and more valuable to me—than hitting any numbers or achieving the goal. In that moment, I made a shift: the personal development shift from goals to growth. The goals I set and achieved were nice, but they weren't as significant as the growth I experienced. Goals helped me to *do* better. But growth helped me to *become* better. The growth experience was giving me greater satisfaction than reaching individual goals.

CONSIDER

Up to now, where have you focused your time and attention—and where have you received your satisfaction—as you've pursued success? In the achievement of your goals or on what you've learned along the way? How do you think your attitude has impacted your life?

_____

_____

_____

_____

_____

GOALS HELPED ME TO *DO* BETTER. BUT GROWTH HELPED ME TO *BECOME* BETTER.

There was also another great benefit. Soon other leaders began asking me how I had accomplished the growth of the church, and I started teaching what I had learned. That was the start of my career as a leadership trainer and speaker. Achieving a goal had opened the door to the opportunity, but my ongoing ability to train others and develop my career as a trainer and speaker came as the fruit of my personal growth. And I've been able to continue speaking because personal development became my focus.

GROWTH CHANGES

As I look back at the time I was making this personal development leadershift from goals to growth, I can see that I made three significant shifts in the way I approached becoming a better leader:

1. GROWTH OUTWARD TO GROWTH INWARD

When I started my career, I was motivated by my desire to meet numerical goals, and every year I set those kinds of goals for myself. I'd look at every area of my career, break each large goal down into smaller, achievable goals, and attack them. I believed that hitting numbers would automatically make me better. And I hoped that external production would increase my internal motivation. But I discovered that it didn't. Instead, the focus on hitting numbers started to wear me down. That prompted me to realize that growth on the inside fuels growth on the outside, not the other way around. I recognized I needed to make a leadershift.

2. GROWTH IN EVERYTHING TO GROWTH IN A FEW VITAL THINGS

When I understood that my focus needed to be internal rather than external, I began thinking about where and how I wanted to grow. That made me realize how unfocused I was. At age twenty-six, my hunger to grow was greater than my willingness to get specific in my areas of growth. If you'd asked me where I wanted to improve, I'd have said, "Everywhere." But it's impossible to grow everywhere all at once. So how would I proceed?

I decided to study success. My desire was to spend a year examining what made people successful and try to discover what all of them had in common. Even as I started this process, I knew what the first quality was: attitude. My father had taught me that. Not a naturally optimistic person, Dad had studied successful people as a youth and found that a positive attitude was something they all had in common. Dad had made it a regular practice to read books that promoted a positive attitude, such as the works of Norman Vincent Peale, and had paid me to read those same books as I was growing up. I would become intentional about continuing to improve in this area.

GROWTH ON THE INSIDE FUELS GROWTH ON THE OUTSIDE.

The second characteristic I quickly attributed to successful people was the ability to develop strong relationships. This was a natural strength of mine. As a teenager I had observed that people go along with people when they get along with them. I liked people and found that they usually responded well to me. So I determined to leverage this natural strength and keep building upon it.

I discovered the third area where I wanted to improve when I read the book *Spiritual Leadership* by J. Oswald Sanders. It helped me understand the impact of good leadership. It was then that I recognized that everything rises and falls on leadership.

The last piece of the success puzzle to fall into place came when I discovered the importance of equipping. In my first leadership position, I had helped my organization to grow, but within six months of my departure, the organization had regressed. I had not equipped a single person to carry on without me.

Since then I've focused my growth on these four key areas, which I later turned into the acronym R-E-A-L so that I could teach it to others: Relationships, Equipping, Attitude, and Leadership. Those are my focus when I read books and articles, listen to podcasts, and attend conferences. Those areas have also become the focus of my teaching and my writing.

CONSIDER

Where do you believe you need to focus your growth? Write at least one but no more than five growth targets for your life.

1. _____
   _____

2. _____
   _____

3. _____
   _____

4. _____
   _____

5. _____
   _____

3. GROWTH WITH A TIMELINE VERSUS GROWTH WITHOUT A FINISH LINE

As a young leader, I was focused on achieving goals. One of the questions I continually asked myself as I set a goal was, *How long will this take?* I'm naturally impatient and I was often preoccupied by how long any given task would take. But as I shifted from goals to growth, my mind-set changed. My thinking shifted onto the bigger picture, and I became less impatient. (I won't say I became *patient* because everyone I know would call me on it!)

As I made this shift, instead of worrying about how long something might take, I started asking, *How far can I go?* Instead of thinking about what I was getting and how much I had to pay to get it, I started to think about who I was becoming and the impact I could make because of it. I recognized I was on a growth journey. And I started to fall in love with personal development. What's more, at age seventy-one, I'm still in love with it.

In my organizations, I try to cultivate that same love. I do that by promoting a culture focused on growth, not goals.

CONSIDER

Take a look at the difference between the two columns below and note which of the two phrases on each line best describes your current focus.

GOAL-ORIENTED CULTURE	GROWTH-ORIENTED CULTURE
☐ Values Achievement	☐ Values Development
☐ Focuses on Status	☐ Focuses on Stretching
☐ Honors Privilege	☐ Honors Serving
☐ Emphasizes the Teacher	☐ Emphasizes the Student
☐ Target Is Arrival	☐ Target Is Growth

The more you can shift your focus from goals to growth, the greater you can increase your potential. Growth is sustaining. Growth is the only guarantee that tomorrow will be better than today.

HOW TO BECOME A GROWTH-ORIENTED PERSON

Making the leadershift from goal-oriented to growth-oriented isn't complicated, but it isn't easy either. It requires a shift in mind-set. It takes time, but it's well worth it. If you shoot for goals, you'll achieve your goals but you may not grow. If you shoot for growth, you'll grow *and* you'll achieve goals. To start making that shift, do these seven things:

1. EMBRACE CHANGE

In 1974 I heard Olan Hendrix, currently the CEO of the Leadership Resource Group, say, "Growth means change." That has always stuck with me, because I think it's human nature to desire improvement and resist change at the same time. And that's impossible.

If you want to become a better leader, a better employee, a better person, you must shift from a fixed mind-set to a growth mind-set. Why?

A Fixed Mind-set	A Growth Mind-set
Believes Intelligence Is Static	Believes Intelligence Can Be Developed
Avoids Challenges	Embraces Challenges
Gives Up Too Easily	Persists When Faced with Setbacks
Sees Effort as Fruitless	Sees Effort as a Path to Mastery
Ignores Constructive Criticism	Learns from Constructive Criticism
Feels Threatened by the Success of Others	Finds Lessons and Inspiration in the Success of Others
Plateaus Early and Achieves Less Than Full Potential	Reaches Higher Levels of Achievement

A fixed mind-set results in an early plateau, achieves less, and hinders people from reaching their full potential, whereas a growth mind-set fuels people to a higher level of achievement. Beverly Sills said, "There are no shortcuts to any place worth going." That's certainly true when it comes to growth. It's a long, slow road, but it's a highly rewarding one. And it requires us to stretch.

CONSIDER

Look at the list describing a growth mindset. Which of the seven actions do you already do well? Why? Which is the most challenging? Why? What can you do to improve in this area?

_____

_____

_____

_____

_____

_____

2. Adopt a Teachable Spirit

Growth begins with having a teachable spirit. What does that entail? It means having a passion to learn, possessing the intention to learn every day, and reflecting on what you learn so that you know how to apply it. It's a bit like gardening. A garden doesn't spring to life on its own. It requires planning, hard work, and the right environment. A gardener must do the work: prepare the soil, plant the seeds, water the plants, then feed, mulch, and weed. It's an intentional process, and it must occur every day.

I try to cultivate a growth environment and maintain a teachable spirit. How do I do that?

- *I Make Growth My Number-One Priority.* I am conscious of my need to learn 24/7 because a day without growth is not a good day for me.

- *I Look for Growth Possibilities in Every Situation.* No matter what I'm doing, whether succeeding or failing, opportunities to grow are there. The question is, do I see it and take advantage of it?

- *I Ask Questions That Will Help Me Grow.* Growth doesn't find me. I must find it. The fastest way to find out what I don't know is to ask questions. The best way to dig deeper and learn more is to ask questions. Are you getting the picture?

- *I File What I Have Learned.* People forget a lot of what they learn. If they want to recall it, they can't. Or they can't find it. When I find articles of value, I clip them and put them in folders by subject. When I find quotes I like, I add them to index cards filed by topic. I file what I learn so that I can always regain access to it quickly.

- *I Pass What I Learn on to Others.* Sharing something that I learn reinforces growth and prompts me to make it my own. It also allows me to help others.

I encourage you to find your own ways to remain teachable and facilitate learning. It will open you up to amazing new possibilities.

CONSIDER

What one habit can you begin practicing today—and every day hereafter—to help you adopt a more teachable spirit?

_____

_____

_____

_____

_____

3. MAKE YOUR LOVE FOR LEARNING GREATER THAN YOUR FEAR OF FAILURE

Over the years, I have experienced the fruits of failure. I don't count my losses; I count the lessons I've learned from them. I wrote *Sometimes You Win, Sometimes You Learn* to help people to learn from their losses. Even failure isn't failure if you learn something from it. That's how you can make failure your friend.

I can remember the day that fear of failure became my friend. It occurred in Los Angeles when I was asked to speak at a conference. Every speaker on the program was more successful, experienced, mature, and recognized than I was. I was less in every way, and I was feeling it. Finally, in the green room, I confided with one of the best speakers.

"I don't feel qualified to be speaking here," I told him. I think I was hoping for reassurance. Instead, his reply startled me.

"You're not," he said. "Speak afraid. Be willing to do it afraid, and eventually you will become qualified."

That was a revelation, and it created a leadershift in me. I spoke afraid, did my best, and here is what I discovered: action reduces fear and increases courage. That realization was a major step toward increasing my love for learning and decreasing my fear of failure.

ACTION REDUCES FEAR AND INCREASES COURAGE.

Don't allow failure to be a bully in your life. It will, if you let it. Many people get intimidated by failure every day. Instead, you need to make failure your friend. How? Fail early, fail often, and fail forward.

TAKE ACTION

What significant task have you been afraid to do that you should work toward starting? What specific action can you take that's the equivalent of "speaking afraid"? When will you take it?

Specific Action: _____

_____

Date: _____

4. DEVELOP RELATIONSHIPS WITH OTHER GROWING PEOPLE

It's much easier to become a growing person if you're in a positive growth environment. I realized this when I was in my twenties, and it inspired me to write out a description of a growth environment. I observed that such environments have ten characteristics. Recently I was looking at this list and I realized that five of the ten involve other people. (I italicized them for emphasis.)

1. *Others are ahead of me.*
2. I am continually challenged.
3. My focus is forward.
4. *The atmosphere is affirming.*
5. I am often out of my comfort zone.
6. I wake up excited.
7. Failure is not my enemy.
8. *Others are growing.*
9. *People desire change.*
10. *Growth is modeled and expected.*

Much of my personal growth has come as a direct result of having the opportunity to spend time with growing people. Elmer Towns, one of the growing people who was a mentor in the formative years of my life, taught me what he called the hot poker principle. He used to say that if you keep the poker near the fire it remains hot. Remove it and over time it becomes cold. He likened growing people to fire and would often remind me, "John, stay close to the fire." That is exactly what I have tried to do.

CONSIDER

Evaluate your environment based on the criteria listed above. Mark your answer beside each statement.

YES	NO	
☐	☐	Others are ahead of me.
☐	☐	I am continually challenged.
☐	☐	My focus is forward.
☐	☐	The atmosphere is affirming.
☐	☐	I am often out of my comfort zone.
☐	☐	I wake up excited.
☐	☐	Failure is not my enemy.
☐	☐	Others are growing.
☐	☐	People desire change.
☐	☐	Growth is modeled and expected.

If you don't have a bunch of yeses lined up, your environment is working against you. What could you do to change or improve this?

_____

_____

_____

_____

_____

5. DEVELOP GREATER HUMILITY

"Humility is not denying your strengths," said pastor and author Rick Warren. "Humility is being honest about your weaknesses." The essence of humility is being unafraid to admit when we're wrong. It's like saying we want to be wiser tomorrow than we are today. And the more we learn and grow, the more we recognize what we don't know.

Leaders who possess humility are confident yet feel no need to draw attention to themselves. They are comfortable with themselves yet acknowledge that they need to improve. They have self-awareness. They gratefully receive criticism. And they are not threatened when others shine. They are happy for them.

Are you willing to be criticized for the sake of improvement? Are you willing to admit you're wrong in deference to your desire to change and grow? Are you willing to drop bad habits, change wrong priorities, and embrace new ways of thinking? That's what it will take to make the leadershift to growth. You must be willing to admit where you're wrong so that you can discover what is right. Anyone can make that choice, but it requires humility.

6. BELIEVE IN YOURSELF

The Law of the Mirror in my book *The 15 Invaluable Laws of Growth* states: "You must see value in yourself to add value to yourself." What you think about yourself determines the investment you will make in yourself. If your self-worth is low, then your investment in yourself will be low. If you see yourself as a two (out of ten), then you'll make a two-level investment. If you see yourself as an eight, you'll make an eight-level investment. That matters because your growth return will not exceed your growth investment.

WHAT YOU THINK ABOUT YOURSELF DETERMINES THE INVESTMENT YOU WILL MAKE IN YOURSELF.

Benjamin Franklin said, "Empty the coins of your purse into your mind and your mind will fill your purse with coins." What a great way to think about it. Be willing to invest in yourself.

7. Embrace Layered Learning

In 1954, politician Adlai Stevenson addressed the senior class at Princeton University. Here, in part, is what he said:

> What a man knows at fifty that he did not know at twenty is, for the most part, incommunicable. The laws, the aphorisms, the generalizations, the universal truths, the parables and the old saws—all the observations about life which can be communicated handily in ready, verbal packages—are as well known to a man at twenty who has been attentive as to a man at fifty. He has been told them all, he has read them all, and he has probably repeated them all before he graduates from college; but he has not lived them all.
>
> What he knows at fifty that he did not know at twenty boils down to something like this: The knowledge he has acquired with age is not the knowledge of formulas, or forms of words, but of people, places, actions—a knowledge not gained by words but by touch, sight, sound, victories, failures, sleeplessness, devotion, love—the human experiences and emotions of this earth and of oneself and other men; and perhaps, too, a little faith, and a little reverence for things you cannot see.[1]

At the time Stevenson made these statements, he was in his mid-fifties, and what he describes is what I would call layered learning—one life lesson applied upon another and another, each gaining greater insight, depth, and weight. It is wisdom acquired and applied over time, and I believe it is the best kind of learning.

If you desire to grow to your maximum potential as a person and a leader, embrace layered learning. As you do, know these things about it:

Layered Learning Requires Time and Intentionality

Any gardener knows you can't force a seed to grow faster than nature intended it to. You can't make trees bear good fruit before they're mature. You can't rush the season. Plants need to grow, and though they may grow every day, it will not show every day. It takes a lot of growing to do a little showing.

That doesn't mean we shouldn't cultivate growth every day. Small improvements over time make a big difference. Knowledge gives us a layer of learning, increasing with each added layer until it turns into wisdom. It takes years, decades, sometimes a lifetime for a person to become an overnight success.

LAYERED LEARNING GIVES YOU A BIGGER PICTURE

Layered learning is like building a picture one piece at a time. It's like receiving additional pieces of the jigsaw puzzle of leadership and putting them in place so that the picture enlarges. What you see becomes more relevant. It also enlarges you as a leader because the more pieces you receive, the better your perspective and the greater your understanding of the principles involved in leadership.

- Layered learning determines the depth of a principle.
- Layered learning determines the length of a principle.
- Layered learning determines the consistency of a principle.
- Layered learning determines the compounding impact of a principle.

You are capable of adding layers and acquiring more of the big picture than you possess today.

LAYERED LEARNING GIVES YOU A BETTER PICTURE

Recently I received the opportunity to revise my book *Developing the Leader Within You* on the occasion of its twenty-fifth anniversary. My publisher requested that I revise at least 15 percent of it so that they could call it a new edition. I relished the thought of updating the book and dove in. By the time I was done, I hadn't rewritten 15 percent; I'd rewritten 85 percent! It changed so much, my publisher decided to call it *Developing the Leader Within You 2.0.*

How was I able to make so many changes to a book that was already highly successful? Layered learning. In the twenty-five years since I had written the original version, I had continued to grow in leadership.

When you make the personal development shift from goals to growth and embrace the process of layered learning, you will never stop getting better. And your level of success can keep expanding.

*   *   *

I like to think of layered learning the way C. S. Lewis talked about learning. He said that learning isn't so much like a train going from one station to the next, so that we leave one place and move on to somewhere else. Instead, our growth is similar to that of a tree. As we learn and grow, we add new rings of understanding without giving up the older ones. We build, using the past to strengthen us. And create something new.[2]

GROWTH PERSPECTIVE

Few things have a greater positive impact than shifting from goals to growth. Why do I say that? Because the benefits are so numerous. Make growth your priority and . . .

- You will unlock and achieve your potential.
- You will feel good about yourself.
- You will strengthen your values and abilities.
- You will grow in humility and self-awareness.
- You will *become* more so you can *do* more.
- You will be an example for others to follow.

I want to say one more thing about shifting from goals to growth before we move on to the next leadershift. Being a goal-oriented person means having more of a short-term mind-set. We often reach for goals because we want the positive feelings that come from quick achievements. But when we make the shift to focusing on growth, it means we've begun to adopt a long-term mind-set. By focusing on growth, we go from improving in spurts to improving day after day to reach our potential. That consistency compounds. And that's important because your level of success will never exceed your level of personal development.

TAKE ACTION

Go back and look at the growth target or targets you wrote earlier in this lesson. Write those targets below along with a plan of specific actions you can take to improve in that area, how you will gauge the evidence of your growth, and the date you desire to accomplish it.

Target 1: _____

Plan: _____
_____
_____

Evidence of Growth: _____

Date: _____

Target 2: _____

Plan: _____
_____
_____

Evidence of Growth: _____

Date: _____

Target 3: _____

Plan: _____
_____
_____

Evidence of Growth: _____

Date: _____

Target 4: _____

Plan: _____

_____

_____

Evidence of Growth: _____

Date: _____

Target 5: _____

Plan: _____

_____

_____

Evidence of Growth: _____

Date: _____

GOALS TO
GROWTH

THE PERSONAL DEVELOPMENT SHIFT

DISCUSSION QUESTIONS

1. What challenges or difficulties do you anticipate facing by changing your focus from external goals to internal growth? What can you do to overcome them?

2. How do you respond intellectually and emotionally to the challenge to grow without a timeline or finish line? Does that excite you or discourage you? Why?

3. What can you do to help yourself love learning more than fear failure? How does belief in yourself come into play?

4. Do you have an example of layered learning you can share from your own life? If so, how did it occur, how did you benefit, and what did you learn that you can apply to future growth?

LESSON FOUR

PERKS TO
PRICE

THE COST SHIFT

Strength and growth come through continuous effort and struggle.

NAPOLEON HILL

I've met a lot of people who desire to become leaders. That's only natural since I do so much teaching and writing on the subject. When I get the chance to interact with people one-on-one, I often ask them why they want to be leaders. Sometimes their answers reveal that their motivation is really about the perks of leading. They want to be in control. They want others to do what they say. They want a nicer office. They want a higher income. They want a better parking place.

When I started out as a young leader, my thoughts were similar. I was enamored with my title of pastor. It conveyed to me that I was the shepherd of the flock, and I thought people would automatically follow me because they needed me. They would rely on me for direction and be grateful for everything I did for them. It seemed simple.

Then reality hit. The people of the church were kind to me, but they didn't automatically follow me. That's when I learned what I later called the Law of E. F. Hutton: when the real leader speaks, people listen. The title that I expected to be so important didn't come with any of the perks I anticipated. I learned that I would have to earn influence myself along the way.

Fifty years later, I can say that in my career as a leader, I've received just about every kind of perk imaginable. I've received titles, recognition, honorary degrees, authority, nice offices, good parking places, money, preferential treatment—you name it, I've had it! However, none of these things motivates me as a leader. I lead because of what I can do for other people. That's the best motivation to lead others. It took time to get there, but I made the shift from being focused on what I can receive as a leader (the perks) to what I can give as a leader (the price).

CONSIDER

Take a look at the kinds of questions leaders ask themselves based on where they focus their attention. Mark the question on each line that most often represents how you think. After you mark them, think about what your answers say about your leadership attitude.

LEADERS WHO FOCUS ON PERKS

- ❑ What will I receive?
- ❑ How will this decision affect me?
- ❑ How long will this take me?
- ❑ What will you give me to stay in the game?

LEADERS WHO FOCUS ON PRICE

- ❑ What can I give?
- ❑ How will this decision affect others?
- ❑ How far can we go?
- ❑ What must I give to stay in the game?

The choice to lead because of benefits, benefits no one, not even the leader. Focusing on perks won't take you anywhere worthwhile because deep inner fulfillment never comes from perks. What they offer is ultimately hollow. And they have never helped a leader to reach his or her potential. Leaders who focus on perks end up misusing their leadership, and because they love perks more than people, they are continually tempted to misuse people to receive, maintain, or improve their perks.

If you want to reach your potential, become the best leader you can be, and make the greatest impact, then you must shift from perks to price in your leadership. A price is what stands between you and your potential. If you want to be a better leader, you need to pay for it.

YOUR PRICE POINTS

While many of the specifics of the price will be unique to each individual leader, there are some common costs that every leader needs to take into account. I want to discuss three that should be part of every leader's shift from perks to price:

1. REALITY—LEADERS RECOGNIZE THAT EVERYTHING WORTHWHILE IS UPHILL

Max De Pree, CEO of the furniture giant Herman Miller, said, "The first responsibility of a leader is to define reality." Let me define the reality of your leadership potential: it's uphill all the way. No one ever coasted to success. No successful person has ever experienced accidental achievements. Nothing of genuine value is easy, quick, and downhill. All the precious things in life require that we pay a price. Contrary to the line in the old song, the best things in life are not free. Or as someone told me once during a break in one of my speeches, "If it doesn't suck, it's not worth doing."

There's a lot of difference between what we can't do and what we won't do. What we *won't* do will keep us from being successful a lot more than what we *can't* do. Poor choices, not lack of talent and ability, are the greatest hindrances to most people's success. If we want to succeed in leadership, we must do what we don't want to do, so we can do what we need to do. We must be willing to pay the price. Early American missionary Adoniram Judson is rumored to have said, "There is no success without sacrifice. If you succeed without sacrifice it is because someone has suffered before you. If you sacrifice without success it is because someone will succeed after."

As a leader, how can you prepare yourself to pay the price required to reach your potential? How do you get ready for the long uphill journey? I think you can learn a lesson from Navy Vice Admiral James Stockdale. In his book *Good to Great*, Jim Collins writes about Stockdale and what Collins calls the Stockdale Paradox.

Stockdale was a pilot who spent eight years imprisoned in North Vietnam's notorious Hanoi Hilton after he was shot down during the Vietnam War. He was frequently tortured and abused. When Collins interviewed Stockdale, the former admiral said his imprisonment was "the defining event of my life," explaining, "I never lost faith in the end of the story. . . . I never doubted not only that I would get out, but also that I would prevail."

Collins was intrigued by this man whose body, decades later, still showed signs of being broken but whose spirit was as indomitable as ever.

"Who didn't make it out?" Collins asked a little hesitantly.

"Oh, that's easy," he said. "The optimists." When a confused Collins asked him to explain, Stockdale said, "Oh, they were the ones who said, 'We're going to be out by Christmas.' And Christmas would come, and Christmas would go. Then they'd say, 'We're going to be out by Easter.' And Easter would come, and Easter would go. And then Thanksgiving, and then it would be Christmas again. And they died of a broken heart."

What Stockdale said next gave Collins the idea for the Stockdale Paradox: "This is a very important lesson. You must never confuse faith that you will prevail in the end—which you can never afford to lose—with the discipline to confront the most brutal facts of your current reality, whatever they might be."[1] Here's how Collins states the Stockdale Paradox:

Retain faith that you will prevail in the end,
    regardless of the difficulties.
AND at the same time
    confront the most brutal facts of your current reality,
    whatever they might be.[2]

These twin expectations of faith and fact help us to believe we can prevail in the end but remind us that the process won't be easy.

I express these twin expectations to myself using different words. As I prepare to lead, I think of *hope* and *hard*. These words help me personally to handle the very different expectations needed for leadership. *Hope* empowers me to believe that I can make the climb. It fuels me with energy to continue when I get tired. And it enables me to speak hope into the lives of the people who are journeying with me. I cannot give hope to others if I do not possess it myself.

It must come from a place of authenticity because you can't fake hope. As you encourage yourself, your people feel that encouragement too. As you encourage them, you also become encouraged. It creates a positive cycle that keeps everyone moving forward.

While I love the encouragement of *hope*, I also value the level-setting word *hard*. It balances my expectations and prevents me from being naively optimistic. I remind myself that the leadership journey is often difficult. Much of success lies in possessing right expectations.

I confess that during the early years of my leadership, I possessed an excess of hope but had very little knowledge or expectation for how hard leading would be. As a result, I set myself and those I led up for disappointment. We expected the best, and that's the only thing we prepared ourselves for. When things got hard and didn't go perfectly, we weren't ready for it. When you don't prepare for the worst, the worst wins!

WHEN YOU DON'T PREPARE FOR THE WORST, THE WORST WINS.

Management consultant and business visionary Peter Drucker said, "A time of turbulence is a dangerous time, but its greatest danger is the temptation to deny reality." As leaders we can't deny reality, nor should we try to sugarcoat it when communicating with our people. We need to bring reality into the conversation as soon as possible. In other words, we should strive to be up-front with the hard part of any journey we plan to take others on.

I used to wait for a good time to share hard realities with others, and then I realized that there's never a good time to share hard news, and the longer I waited, the harder it was to talk about it. Since then I've made it a regular practice to look for and mention any downside to a process I'm trying to communicate. I want people to know there is a price to pay for progress.

No matter what you want to do in life, you have to face reality, and you have to be willing to pay the price required to go uphill. The sooner you start climbing and the more you're willing to pay, the higher you can go.

CONSIDER

There are leadership goals you have abandoned and important tasks you avoid because you have told yourself you can't achieve them. What if those tasks aren't really *can'ts*? What if they are actually *won'ts*? Make a list of leadership hopes, dreams, and aspirations you once possessed that have fallen to the wayside.

_____

_____

_____

_____

_____

_____

_____

_____

Now do some serious soul-searching. Which of those one-time desires is really something you are not pursuing because you don't want to pay the price? Sometimes that decision is good and right. Sometimes it isn't. Which of the items on your list should you pick back up and pursue again? Mark them.

2. EXAMPLE—LEADERS ACKNOWLEDGE THEY MUST CLIMB THE HILL FIRST

All people with leadership ability have one perspective in common: before and more. They see things *before* other people do, and they see *more* than other people do. However, what sets great leaders apart from all other leaders is this: they *act before* others and they *do more* than others. Great leaders face their uncertainty and doubt, and they move through it to pave the way for others. And because they are willing to pay the price first and often pay more than others do, they can say with moral authority, "Follow me."

When times are tough and challenges are difficult, being first isn't a perk. It's a cost that has to be paid. In the uphill climb to achieving something worthwhile, leaders have to pay that price by climbing first and leading the way. There is no elevator to the top. Someone has to find the path and set the example.

**WHAT SETS GREAT LEADERS APART FROM ALL OTHER LEADERS IS THIS:
THEY *ACT BEFORE* OTHERS AND THEY *DO MORE* THAN OTHERS.**

A person's title or position doesn't help here. The climb isn't enhanced by college degrees. Or material possessions. No one is inspired by any of those things. It's the actions leaders take that inspire others to follow and to rally to the vision. Great leaders take action. They move out front, staying ahead but within sight of their people, and they say, "follow me." The example of a good leader continually inspires people.

Follow-me leaders know it's their responsibility to set the example. Over the years, I've observed that they share three common before-and-more characteristics:

FOLLOW-ME LEADERS BELIEVE IN THEMSELVES BEFORE AND MORE THAN OTHERS DO

I've observed a lot of successful people whom others have not believed in, but I've yet to meet a successful person who did not believe in him- or herself. Self-belief comes first. As leaders, we cannot give to others what we do not possess ourselves.

Self-belief is more than saying positive words to myself or receiving them from others. As radio broadcaster Paul Harvey said, "If you don't live it, you don't believe it." Words of affirmation without the work of accomplishment are hollow. Even if others believe in you, their borrowed belief must be activated by success and become self-belief if it is to be sustained. Borrowed belief without results soon loses its power. A leader's self-belief must be authentic, and it must be backed up with successful action.

FOLLOW-ME LEADERS SET EXPECTATIONS FOR THEMSELVES BEFORE AND MORE THAN OTHERS DO

Leaders are in trouble when they need someone else to set the level of expectations. If that continues, they will cease to lead others. Sadly, there are a lot of people who go in the opposite direction, trying to do as little as they can to stay afloat in their careers. It's like they're treading water in the pool during an Olympic swimming race.

If you want to be a good leader, you must have high expectations for yourself. I like the advice given by Dianne Snedaker, executive vice president and chief marketing officer of First Republic Bank, who said:

> Set your standards high and keep them high. If you are interested in success, it's easy to set your standards in terms of other people's accomplishments. And then let other people measure you by those standards. But the standards you set for yourself are always the more important. They should be higher than the standards anyone else would set for you, because in the end you have to live with yourself, and judge yourself, and feel good about yourself. And the best way to do that is to live up to your highest potential. So set your standards high and keep them high, even if you think no one else is looking. Somebody out there will always notice, even if it's just you.[3]

You can't set a low standard of performance for yourself and expect to lead others effectively.

Follow-Me Leaders Make Commitments to Themselves Before and More Than to Others

To be successful, leaders must continually make commitments. Commitment is key. But the first and most important commitment that any leader makes is to him- or herself: a commitment to integrity, responsibility, and selflessness. Good leaders promise themselves they will pay the price and follow through regardless of the circumstances.

One of the leaders I most admire is Abraham Lincoln. Before Lincoln became president, few people expected him to be one of the nation's greatest leaders. In fact, the *New York Times* said he was unqualified for the presidency of the United States. But Lincoln was committed to helping the nation. He later revealed his mind-set of commitment: "I have never done an official act with a view to promote my own personal aggrandizement, and I don't like to begin now."[4]

* * *

If you're a leader, or you desire to become one, you must always be ready, willing, and committed to climbing the hill first. Climb first, setting the example, and call out "follow me." If you're willing to do that, there's still one more quality you must display as you pay the price of leadership.

CONSIDER

Think about the leadership example you set for others by answering these three questions:

Do you believe in yourself before and more than others do? (If so, what examples of belief can you list as evidence? If not, how must you change?)

_____

_____

_____

_____

_____

Do you set expectations for yourself before and more than others do? (If so, what examples of expectations for yourself can you list as evidence? If not, how must you change?)

_____

_____

_____

_____

_____

Do you make commitments to yourself before and more than to others? (If so, what examples of commitment can you list as evidence? If not, how must you change?)

_____

_____

_____

_____

3. CONSISTENCY—LEADERS UNDERSTAND THEY NEVER GET TO STOP CLIMBING

I have another confession to make. Early in my leadership, I thought that if I led well for a season, I could earn the right to take shortcuts and quit making sacrifices. I thought I could pay the price for a little while, be done paying, and then enjoy the good life—the perks that came with having paid a price. That created a blind spot in my leadership and led to "destination disease." I thought I could arrive at a time, place, and situation that would give me the greatest of all perks—recognition without responsibility.

There is no such place—unless you get out of the game. But I don't want out of the game. I'm more than seventy years old, and I still like the game. What I've discovered is that I had to give up to go up, and I have to give up even more if I want to stay up!

There is a reason that sports teams seldom have back-to-back championships. The perks that come with the first championship often become a hindrance to achieving the next one. When a team earns the first championship, they don't get the next one free. Dwight D. Eisenhower, whose leadership experience included serving as both a general and the president of the United States, said, "There is no victory at bargain basement prices."

If you desire to go to higher levels of leadership, you need to keep paying the price. That price will be higher than you think, and it will have to be paid continually and consistently. Jim Collins said, "The signature of mediocrity is chronic inconsistency." A corollary to that would be that the signature of excellence is relentless consistency. But excellence doesn't show up quickly. And you have to work at it to sustain it. Here are some of the ways consistency will help you as a leader.

CONSISTENCY PROVIDES SECURITY FOR OTHERS

Anthropologist Margaret Mead observed, "What people say, what they do, and what they say they do are entirely different things." If you're consistent as a leader, that should not be true of you. Your words, intentions, and actions should all line up. People know where you stand and how you deliver. Others can depend on you, which is perhaps the highest compliment you can receive as a leader.

CONSISTENCY ESTABLISHES YOUR REPUTATION

Just about everyone can be good every once in a while. It's more difficult to be good every time. Consistency lifts people above the crowd and sets them apart.

It can make you someone that others notice. And that's important in leadership because the people you lead are always watching you. When you deliver time after time, you develop a reputation for coming through when needed. Not only does that help you to influence people, it also sets the tone for your team. People do what people continually see. The more consistent you are, the more consistent they will want to be.

CONSISTENCY KEEPS YOU IN THE LEADERSHIP GAME

When you're consistent, it means never having to restart or get back "into the swing of things." You're already swinging. Your constant progress keeps morale high, keeps enthusiasm brimming, and increases your investment in whatever goal you're pursuing. Author and speaker Michael Angier said, "If you develop the habits of success, you'll make success a habit." If you consistently stay on top of your game, you never have to gear up to get back into the game.

CONSISTENCY COMPOUNDS

What did genius Albert Einstein call the greatest mathematical discovery of all time? Not Arabic numerals. Not calculus. Not the theory of relativity. Compound interest—wealth that grows based on continual reinvestment. And what's the secret to compound interest? Consistency! It never stops growing.

One of my favorite examples of the compounding power of consistency occurred in the world of professional baseball in the 1980s and '90s with Cal Ripken Jr. He is in the Hall of Fame, but he isn't there because he was the best hitter, best fielder, or best base stealer. He's there because of consistency.

Ripken played in 2,632 consecutive games, the major league baseball record by a long shot. Only one other player passed the 2,000 mark: Lou Gehrig, with 2,160. For more than forty years, baseball fans believed Gehrig's record would never be broken. The rarity of that kind of consistency becomes clearer when you recognize that only five other players in major league history have ever played in more than a thousand consecutive games. Maybe that's why the game in which Ripken passed Gehrig's record was voted the most memorable in MLB history, ahead of Gehrig's farewell speech in 1939, ahead of Hank Aaron's home run record, and ahead of Jackie Robinson breaking the color barrier in 1947.[5]

Ripken was quick to say that his success didn't come from being more talented than everyone else. When asked if he was a superstar, he responded, "Superstar?

Oh, no. . . . I don't think I stack up with the great talents in the league. I have talent, no doubt. My advantage is that I know the game well." Years later, Ripken said of his record:

> The streak was really born out of a very simple and honest approach. Dad always taught me to show up at the ballpark each and every day ready to play, and if the manager believes you are one of the nine guys who can help the team win that day, he knows he can count on you and will put you in the lineup. That's simply how the streak started and grew over the years.[6]

In other words, he showed up, worked hard, played hurt, and gave his best—every day for sixteen years straight. He was the definition of consistency.

ASSESS

In what area of your leadership are you highly consistent? What has made that consistency possible?

_____

_____

_____

_____

In what area of your leadership would you receive the greatest benefit if you became more consistent? How would it help you? What can you change immediately to pay the price of greater consistency in this area?

_____

_____

_____

_____

_____

_____

_____

* * *

Recently I was backstage before a speaking engagement, waiting to be introduced to the audience. The host described me as "an amazing leader." I mention this only because I know I'm not amazing. Rather, I'm experienced as a leader, and I've stayed consistent. I'm just experiencing the compounding effect of having paid the price to improve as a leader for a really long time. So at this point in my career, I look better than I actually am.

If you want to have an amazing impact as a leader, you need to make the shift from perks to price and do many unamazing things as you make the difficult uphill climb of leadership and set the example for your team. The reality is that:

- Practicing is not amazing.
- Studying is not amazing.
- Showing up is not amazing.
- Working hard is not amazing.
- Asking questions is not amazing.
- Changing is not amazing.
- Trying is not amazing.
- Failing is not amazing.
- Trying again is not amazing.

But every one of these things is necessary. They are the price you must pay every day to reach your potential. If you pay that price and do it consistently, the final result can be amazing.

PERKS TO
PRICE

THE COST SHIFT

DISCUSSION QUESTIONS

1. What is your earliest memory of wanting to become a leader? What motivated you?

2. What motivates your leadership now? Would you assess that motivation as positive, negative, or mixed? Explain.

3. How do you respond to the expectation that you must always set the example for your team and go first in the unpleasant tasks? How do you handle that responsibility?

4. How well do you balance faith that you will prevail with willingness to confront the brutal facts? Which is easier for you? How do you keep doing the other?

5. How well have you embraced the idea that leaders should never stop climbing? Explain. What are the results of your perspective? What must you do to change?

LESSON FIVE

PLEASING PEOPLE TO
CHALLENGING PEOPLE

THE RELATIONAL SHIFT

You cannot lead people if you need people.

Pleasing people is not the same as leading people. That was one of the first important lessons I had to learn in leadership. It defined a new reality for me, and it was very difficult for me to learn. Early in my life I realized that most people liked me. My relational connections with others were strong. My teachers liked me. Kids wanted to hang out with me and be around me in the classroom and on the playground. Intuitively, I knew what mattered to people and was able to please them. So naturally, I worked hard at developing my people-pleasing skills. I felt like my leadership mojo was making everyone happy. And doing it made *me* happy.

During those early years, I might have defined leadership as, "Make people happy and they will follow you." I was continually asking myself one question: "Is everybody happy?" But if you're a leader, the answer is no. You can never make *everyone* happy. And wanting to do so is a setup for disappointment or failure.

WHO NEEDS A WAKE-UP CALL?

I started my professional leadership career at the age of twenty-two. As already mentioned, I was the leader of a small congregation in Indiana. For the first six months, I felt that everybody was happy. The people there liked me, and I liked them. It was all kum-ba-ya.

Then one day I created trouble in paradise. There was an ugly painting in the small lobby of the church. I had noticed it before and thought about how it needed to go, but it hadn't been a priority. I didn't say anything about it to anyone, but I got around to removing it. I considered it a small improvement that I was glad to make.

The reaction was immediate and negative. You'd have thought that I called somebody's baby ugly. Right away I learned that two members of the congregation had given that painting as a gift to the church and had placed it in a prominent spot themselves. When they learned that I had removed it, to say they were not happy is a gross understatement.

I quickly apologized and put the painting back. Whew! That was close. I had dodged the bullet and gone from bad leader to good leader because everyone was happy again.

But a few weeks later, I faced another problem. The youth of our church were playing in a basketball game, and I had promised to attend. But then a member of the church called me with an emergency situation, and I missed the game. The coach of our team and a few of the parents were not happy about it. Uh-oh. I needed do something. So I explained the situation, and the parents got happy again.

But the coach still wasn't happy.

I went to work pleasing him. I visited him twice to smooth things over. And attended the next two games, even though I hadn't promised to. Finally, I had won him back over to the happy side. Yay. I'd succeeded. But boy was this happy stuff beginning to wear me out. How could I possibly keep up with making everybody happy?

For two years I did everything I could to try to make everyone I led happy. I sincerely believed that if my leadership was good, everybody would like me and everything I did. And if someone—anyone—didn't like me or something I did, then it must mean there was something wrong with my leadership and I needed to fix it. That thinking motivated every action I took and every decision I made.

What a mistake! No leader can please everyone all the time. Even history's greatest leaders had their opponents. But back then, I hadn't yet realized that. When the reality struck me that *everyone* wasn't happy *all* the time, I hit an emotional wall. I believed that I was a bad leader, and I even wondered if I should resign from my position and try to lead somewhere else.

But then I got wise counsel from leaders with more experience. They helped me to understand that it's impossible to please everyone. Then they taught me an even more important insight about myself. I was doing things backward. My goal had been to get people to like me enough so that I could gain the confidence to ask them for commitment. If they declined, I simply worked harder to try to get them to like me more, thinking that would solve the problem. Worse still, I gave the most time and energy to the unhappiest and least-committed people, even though they were not contributing to the vision or helping to move the organization forward. I was letting the tail wag the dog.

I finally realized that I wasn't leading people. I was trying to make them and myself feel good. I wasn't moving the organization forward. I was in the friendship business, not the leadership business. I wasn't taking people anywhere or helping them to do better and get better. I was trying to live in Happyville.

To get the best out of people, leaders must ask for the best from people. I wasn't doing that at all. Once I realized this, I wish I could say that I shifted from pleasing people to challenging people quickly and easily, but I can't. The process of change for me was very slow. My desire to be liked by others was deeply rooted within me to the point where my best days in leadership were the ones when people affirmed me. I craved that affirmation every day. But I recognized that affirmation doesn't equal leadership accomplishment, so I vowed to change. Step by step, I talked myself out of the idealistic thoughts and feelings I had as a young leader and coached myself to try to become the leader that the people really needed, not just the one they wanted. I made the leadershift from pleasing people to challenging them.

HOW TO SHIFT FROM PLEASER TO LEADER

I don't know whether you have the people-pleasing tendencies I once had. If so, you need to make the same leadershift I did, because you can never really lead your organization, serve your people, or reach your leadership potential if you're always trying to make others happy. You have to put *doing* what's right for your people and organization ahead of what *feels* right for you. To make that shift, you need to do these seven things:

1. CHANGE YOUR EXPECTATIONS TOWARD LEADERSHIP

I had to change the way I thought about leadership and the way I interacted with others to become a good leader. I had to stop seeking affirmation. I had to stop trying to be everyone's buddy. One of the people who helped me improve in this area was my mentor, Fred Smith (the consultant, not the founder of FedEx). Once while we were discussing how to handle difficult situations with people, he said, "Always separate what's best for you from what's best for the organization." That statement felt like a smack in the face, because too often I had put myself first. I had always thought about what was best for me. Fred gave me a new perspective and suggested that I think about things in a different order:

1. What's best for the organization?
2. What's best for other people within the organization?
3. What's best for me?

By learning to ask myself these three questions in this order, I was able to clarify my motives for leadership decisions.

CONSIDER

When you have to make leadership decisions, what is the order of your thinking? How does it impact your effectiveness as a leader? What, if anything, needs to change for you to better serve your organization and team?

_____

_____

_____

_____

_____

_____

I must say that during this relational leadershift from pleasing people to challenging people, I felt great loneliness as a leader. The affirmation that had been such a wonderful sound to my ears went silent during this season. The people who used to seek me out for consensus avoided me when they were unhappy. Some of the people who used to "toast" me now wanted to "roast" me. But as I stepped back from the crowd, I started to find myself. I discovered that if I *needed* people, I probably couldn't lead them well. That gave me determination to shift from making them happy to helping them get better.

Eventually I began to desire what was best for the people, I felt released to do the right thing as a leader. I shared the vision, raised the bar, challenged others, showed the way, asked for commitment, and stopped waiting for consensus. The organization was able to take ground, and I was able to help people start reaching their God-given potential. Those who didn't want to go with me, I allowed to go their own way without expending all my energy trying to win them back.

One of the greatest lessons I learned in this season was that you never know if people are really with you until you ask them for commitment. When you ask others for commitment, you lose the uncommitted people and you gain the committed ones. When you don't ask for commitment, you keep the uncommitted and lose the committed. You choose who you lose.

> **YOU NEVER KNOW IF PEOPLE ARE REALLY WITH YOU
> UNTIL YOU ASK THEM FOR COMMITMENT.**

If your leadership is motivated by pleasing others or receiving approval, you need to change your expectations. Shift your focus from what you gain to how you can help people, improve your organization, and achieve your vision. Otherwise, your leadership will always be limited.

2. VALUE PEOPLE AS MUCH AS YOU VALUE YOURSELF

Valuing people is a high priority in my life; every day I intentionally add value to others. For me, this always starts with valuing myself. We see others as we see ourselves, and if we value ourselves, we are able to value others.

Your value assessment of yourself determines your personal investment in others. If you feel that you are worthy of opportunity, you will give others opportunities. If you feel that you are worthy of being developed, you will be willing to develop others. If you see yourself as a 9 (out of 10), you will be more likely to value others highly. If you devalue yourself, you will probably devalue others too. And that's critical because you can't devalue others and be a good leader. To get the best out of people, you need to *believe* the best about people. Only then will you give them your best—and ask them to give you their best.

3. WORK TO ESTABLISH EXPECTATIONS UP FRONT

In my people-pleasing years, I never established expectations up front. I'd tell myself that sometime, somewhere, somehow, I'd broach the topic of expectations *when the time was right*. But the time was never right, and I never initiated those conversations. Instead, I would work hard to win people over relationally, hoping that they would guess what I wanted from them and that when the tough times came, they would hang with me. But assumptions are never a good method of operation in the leadership world. They always lead to unfulfilled expectations and disappointment.

As a leader, you can either set expectations on the front end and set up the working relationships for success, or you can leave expectations unstated and deal with disappointment on the back end for both you and the people you're leading.

Today, I see the sharing and setting of expectations on the front end as the litmus test for a leader. I go out of my way to be up-front with people.

- Up-front *appreciation* places value on the person and increases the value of our time together.
- Up-front *expectations* increase the value of any meeting. (The sooner I set expectations, the quicker and easier the meeting.)
- Up-front *questions* are the quickest way for people to understand one another and increase the value of our time together.
- Up-front *discussion* influences the way and direction we lead others.
- Up-front *decisions* increase the value of our time together.

Being up-front means you're out in front.

When I am preparing to have an up-front conversation with someone, I work to level-set the interaction with one question and seven statements. First, the question:

WHAT ARE YOUR EXPECTATIONS FOR OUR INTERACTION?

When I have a conversation with someone, I always invite the other person to go first. It's not only polite but it's smart. Asking a good question without a slanted preamble is good because you can find out what the other person is really thinking, and that's more important than what I want them to think. In addition, if I listen first, the odds increase for the other person to listen to me, because he or she has already been heard.

When I start a professional relationship with someone, the most important thing to establish up-front is our expectations for each other. What does the other person expect of me? What do I expect of him or her? That way we can find out if our desires are compatible. We may need to adjust our expectations to bring them into alignment so that we can both sign off on them. And if I'm the leader in this relationship, the better I know the person, the better I'll know how to lead them.

Once I've learned the other person's expectations up front by asking questions, I set expectations for the other person by communicating these statements:

IT'S NOT ABOUT ME—IT'S NOT ABOUT YOU—IT'S ABOUT THE BIG PICTURE

A mature person has the ability to see and respect different perspectives. However, when you're leading a team, department, or organization, you must always keep your eye on the big picture. To fulfill the bigger picture, no individuals—not any team member and not the leader—can lose sight of the goal and get consumed by themselves.

YOU MUST VALUE OTHER PEOPLE

All leaders are in the people business. If we want to work well with people, we need to value them and add value to them. And here's the good news: adding value to people is also good for business.

Anyone who works with me needs to value people. That's the core of who I am and it's the core of all my companies. We must be willing to serve others, and servant leadership isn't difficult if we value people. When we value people, they feel valued. And we are able to succeed in our mission.

You Are Expected to Keep Growing

How do you grow an organization? Through the growth of its individual members. The future of any organization can be found in the growth of the people who are a part of it, and especially the people who lead it. As the Law of the Lid says, leadership ability determines a person's level of effectiveness.

I am a lifelong learner who is intentional about learning something every day of my life. And I expect anyone who joins my team to be intentional about personal and professional growth. Growing together is even better than growing alone. Teams either grow together or they grow apart. Making a commitment to grow every day and then developing relationships with growing people will keep us on the growth track.

You Must Be Prepared to Change

There is a vast difference between conceding that change is inevitable and believing change is essential. The person who concedes that change is inevitable becomes resigned to it and is reactive, thinking, *Change is going to happen, so what can I do?* The individual who believes change is essential is proactive and thinks, *I will make change happen so that our team can improve.*

> **THERE IS A VAST DIFFERENCE BETWEEN CONCEDING THAT CHANGE IS INEVITABLE AND BELIEVING CHANGE IS ESSENTIAL.**

Everyone Has to Earn My Time

There are a lot of things I freely give to everyone in my organizations: vision, belief, resources, support, and leadership. One thing that must always be earned is my time. That is the most limited of my personal resources, so it must be earned before I give it. How does someone do that? By being a productive member on the team. In this, I practice the 80-20 principle. I give 80 percent of my time to the 20 percent of the team that produces 80 percent of the results.

Always Take Responsibility

Most people want empowerment when what they need first are responsibility and accountability. As Kevin Turner, who is vice chairman of the board of managers of Albertsons and senior advisor to the company's chairman and CEO, said, "People want to be judged by their intentions not by their actions." But results are what make a difference, not good intentions. And results come only when people take responsibility for themselves.

I like what business executive Seth Godin said about this:

Employees wait to be picked for promotion, or to lead a meeting or to speak up at a meeting.

"Pick me, pick me" acknowledges the power of the system and passes responsibility to someone to initiate. Even better, "pick me, pick me" moves the blame from you to them.

If you don't get picked, it's their fault, not yours.

If you do get picked, well, they said you were good, right? Not your fault anymore.

Reject the tyranny of picked. Pick yourself."[1]

That's what taking responsibility is. It's picking yourself. It's motivating yourself. It's bringing intentionality and energy to everything you do.

We Will Not Avoid Tough Conversations

Leadership demands that we tackle the problems. That includes tough conversations. And their difficulty increases when the issue is not easy and it involves people on our team. But we should never delay tough conversations. The more you wait, the more difficult they become. Why?

- Silence to most people means approval.
- When people have to fill in the blanks themselves, they do so negatively.
- Problems left unaddressed have a snowball effect: they become larger and gain momentum.
- Problems left unaddressed cause inner erosion: we lose respect for ourselves internally.

- The Law of Diminishing Intent is in effect: The longer you wait to do something you should do now, the greater the odds that you will never do it. One of these days becomes none of these days.

You've probably heard the saying that all's well that ends well. I also believe that all's well that begins well. That's what establishing up-front expectations does for you as a leader. It helps you begin well so that you can challenge people to become their best.

CONSIDER

What expectations should you be establishing with the people you lead? Write out the questions and statements you need to use with your team members to establish a better working relationship with them so that you can lead them well and challenge them to become their best.

_____

_____

_____

_____

_____

_____

_____

Use this list whenever a new person joins your team. You may also want to sit down individually with current team members, apologize for not having done this sooner, and go over your list with them.

4. ASK YOURSELF THE HARD QUESTIONS BEFORE ANY POTENTIALLY DIFFICULT CONVERSATION

As I grew in my leadershift from pleasing people to challenging people, I had to work hard at becoming better at difficult conversations. One of the questions I began asking myself was, *What is the source of the problem prompting the need for this challenging conversation? Is it an external issue, is it a problem within the other person, or is it me?* If the issue was external, like poor communication, a bad system, or an external problem, it would be easy to solve. If it was a problem related to the person's attitude or actions, it would be more difficult. If the fault was mine, then I might not need to meet with the other person at all. I just needed to own up to it and fix myself! If it was any combination of the three, then the conversation would be very difficult because of the complexity.

As you think about any difficult conversation you are getting ready to have, I want to give you some help. Here is a checklist I've used *before* having difficult conversations to help me prepare:

Questions to Consider:	Yes	No
Have I invested in the relationship enough to be candid with them?		
Do I demonstrate that I value them as individuals?		
Am I sure this is their issue and not mine?		
Am I sure I'm not speaking up because I feel threatened?		
Is the issue more important than the relationship?		
Does this conversation clearly serve their interests and not just mine?		
Am I willing to invest time and energy to help them change?		
Am I willing to show them how to do something and not just say what's wrong?		
Am I willing and able to set clear, specific expectations?		
Have I previously addressed the issue or problem in a less formal setting?		
Total:		

Take a look at the tally of *yes* or *no* responses. If you have one or more *no* responses to any of these questions, consider what steps you need to take to make that *no* become a *yes* before you conduct that crucial conversation.

TAKE ACTION

The next time you need to address a problem you're having with a team member, use the list above to make sure you're prepared for the conversation.

5. WHEN A TOUGH CONVERSATION IS NEEDED, DO IT RIGHT

Because it was once so difficult for me, I want to give you some advice about how to make a tough conversation less tough. First, remember why you are having the conversation. It's because you care about the other person; you care enough to confront them. Your goal is to help that person.

Having the right attitude is essential because your actions often carry more weight than your words, and a negative attitude can cause more damage. People remember how they felt long after they have forgotten what you said. You can communicate the right attitude by seeking to understand. Here is a road map for the conversation:

- State the issue clearly at the beginning. Use the phrase, "Are you aware that . . . ?"
- Ask them to tell you their perspective. Start with the phrase, "I need you to help me understand your situation."
- Ask questions. Say, "Am I hearing you correctly?"
- Repeat back what you heard.
- Allow them to respond.
- Try to find common ground.
- Arrive at an agreement on what's best for both of you.
- If you cannot come to an agreement on the issue and solution, agree to meet again.
- See the growth opportunity that lies within the tough conversation.
- Seek to maintain a positive relationship.

Following this pattern and arriving at a positive outcome is not always possible, but it's worth trying to attain. You're always better off having the tough conversation and finding out where you stand rather than avoiding it and hoping the problem will resolve itself, because it never does.

TAKE ACTION

Use the previous bullet list to guide you the next time you need to have a difficult conversation with a team member.

6. UNDERSTAND THE 25-50-25 PRINCIPLE

Good leadership always challenges people to rise to the occasion, become their best, and achieve more. Some people accept the challenge and help the team to win. Others don't. As a leader, you have to manage the process that people go through. You can use the 25-50-25 principle to help you. I learned about it years ago when I attended a leadership roundtable in Los Angeles.

Here's how it goes: Whenever you cast vision and challenge people to become part of achieving an endeavor, they tend to fall into one of three groups. Typically, 25 percent of the people will support your efforts, 50 percent will be undecided, and 25 percent will resist change. Your job is to help the middle 50 percent join the first 25 percent. Here are tips for doing that and working with all three groups:

- Understand that the resistant bottom 25 percent are not going to join you, no matter what you try to do. The greatest leader in the world could be leading them, and they would still resist change. Accept that.
- Don't waste your effort trying to make this bottom 25 percent happy. They are not going to get happy. Trying to placate them will only encourage their resistance.
- Don't give the bottom 25 percent a platform or credibility. If you believe you're doing the right thing, why would you help them undermine that?

- Try to keep the bottom 25 percent away from the 50 percent who have not yet made up their minds. As baseball manager Casey Stengel said, "The secret of managing is to keep the guys who hate your guts away from the guys who haven't made up their minds yet."
- Ask the 25 percent who support you to help positively influence the middle 50 percent who are undecided.
- Give the supportive 25 percent credibility and a platform to speak. They will help you help the organization move forward.

Any movement you can create in the middle 50 percent toward your leadership and the vision is a win because it takes the organization in the right direction. Celebrate that and keep moving forward.

CONSIDER

How can you apply the 25-50-25 Principle in your organization? Is there an initiative or project where this dynamic is in play? What specific actions can you take to minimize the damage done by the bottom 25 percent?

_____

_____

_____

_____

_____

_____

_____

_____

7. BALANCE CARE WITH CANDOR

I want to give you one more piece of advice related to challenging people, and it's an important one. As a leader, you need to bring both caring and candor into the relationship. I mention this because most people naturally default to one or the other. But here's why it's important for you to practice both:

- Care without candor creates dysfunctional relationships.
- Candor without care creates distant relationships.
- Care balanced with candor creates developing relationships.

Care and candor are like the two wings of a plane; you can't fly with only one. They must work together.

Care	Candor
Values the Person	Values the Person's Potential
Establishes the Relationship	Expands the Relationship
Shores Up Weaknesses	Brings Out Strengths
Offers Comfort	Offers a Challenge
Makes the Team Pleasant	Makes the Team Productive

Caring should never suppress candor, while candor should never displace caring. When I have the responsibility for leading people, I must care for them, but I must also challenge them by initiating honest conversations to help them improve. My mind-set should be, "I love you too much to let you stay where you are."

CONSIDER

Which is most natural for you: caring for others or speaking with candor? How can you improve in the area that comes less naturally to you?

_____

_____

_____

_____

_____

_____

_____

_____

_____

It's been almost fifty years since I made the leadershift from pleasing people to challenging them. It's been one of the most difficult changes I've had to make in my leadership, but it has also been one of the most rewarding. If I hadn't been willing to face up to the need to change, I'd have gotten stuck in my leadership.

I don't know how much difficulty people pleasing has given you. Maybe it's not an issue at all. I hope that's the case. But no matter what, you need to learn how to positively challenge people if you desire to become the best leader you can be. If you can help people to positively reach their potential, you help them, your team, and yourself.

PLEASING PEOPLE TO
CHALLENGING PEOPLE

THE RELATIONAL SHIFT

DISCUSSION QUESTIONS

1. The quote at the beginning of the chapter says, "You cannot lead people if you need people." What is your interpretation of that? Do you agree or disagree? Explain.

2. What is the value of challenging people? Can you share an example of when you were challenged by a leader, and it helped you?

3. Can you share an example of when you challenged someone on your team and the outcome was positive? What strategy did you use with the person and why?

4. When having to make a decision, especially a decision related to people, how do you go about analyzing what's best for the organization, for the people, and for yourself? What criteria do you use for each area?

5. Is there a tough conversation you need to have that you've been putting off? How can you use care and candor to help you have that conversation? When will you initiate it?

NOTES

LESSON SIX

MAINTAINING TO
CREATING

THE ABUNDANCE SHIFT

The joy is in creating—not maintaining.

VINCE LOMBARDI

Have you ever thought about the expectations your profession or industry places on you? Are people in your leadership position expected to hold the line? Maintain the course? Change direction? Get out of the box? Blow up the box?

When I started my career, it never occurred to me to think about such things. I knew from a fairly early age that I was going to become a pastor. That determined my course of study in college, and after I graduated, I was happy to get my first job in rural Indiana. A few weeks after Margaret and I got married, we moved there and I started my career. That was back in 1969. In those days, the role of pastors was pretty set. We were expected to be shepherds, and our main job was to feed and care for the flock. The whole mind-set was *maintaining*. As much as I loved the people in my congregation and had looked forward to being a pastor, it wasn't long before I started to feel unsettled.

Each year the organization I belonged to held a meeting for the pastors and leaders of all the churches. Toward the end of my first year on the job, I went to my initial meeting as the leader of my own church. It was good to see some friends from college and to catch up with them. But what struck me most was how *traditional* everything was. The highlight of the meeting was when the pastor of the year was recognized. For the first time, it struck me. The people they honored were always the ones with the longest tenure, the leaders who were faithful—the maintainers, not the innovators.

I did not want to be a maintainer. Tenure wasn't my goal. I began to feel like a misfit among a group of people who valued tradition and conformity, and my sense of unsettledness only increased. And the way the organization worked was if you were a faithful shepherd at a small church and didn't rock the boat, you were eventually invited to pastor a larger church. If you were faithful there, you would get offered a denominational position. The recognized pastors maintained their way to the top. And on it went until you received recognition toward the end of your career as you approached retirement. I could see the whole path ahead of me. I was beginning to suspect that it wasn't a good fit for me. I wanted to innovate. I wanted to reach people. I wanted to build a great church.

Years later, someone in the ministry world pointed out that not all pastors are actually shepherds. He referred instead to another analogy: church leader as rancher. He described the difference this way: while shepherds are maintainers who care for the sheep they already have, ranchers are leaders who pioneer new ideas and build. Now, I'm not saying that people are livestock. But there's a difference in mind-set between these two types of people, and it was clear which type I was. I wanted to build.

There's an old saying: don't tear down a fence until you know why it's there. Within my organization, I wasn't someone who was itching to tear down fences, but I *was* a questioner. I was very quick to ask why a fence had been put up. And whether it still needed to be there. And if it could be replaced by something better. If the reason something was done was reasonable, then I'd leave it alone. If not, then I started asking, "Why not do it another way—a better way?"

Asking questions and exploring ignited my creativity. Although, within my organization, it seemed like I was the only one doing that. In fact, my questions annoyed them. They questioned my questions—they couldn't understand *why* I was asking them at all. It eventually became clear to me that I wasn't compatible with the culture, and I needed to make a change. So after several years, I left the organization.

Recognize What Zone You're In

I don't want to put down the organization I was a part of or the people I grew up with. They were good people. However, I believe the culture they were part of was working against them. It's difficult overcoming a maintaining culture. And if you also happen to have an inherent tendency toward inactivity when it comes to innovation, you have even more to overcome.

I've observed that we all tend to fall into one of four different zones when it comes to innovation, which impacts how we live, how we lead, and what we achieve. Here are the zones, along with attitude statements that represent them:

1. *The Coasting Zone*—"I do as little as possible."
2. *The Comfort Zone*—"I do what I have always done."
3. *The Challenge Zone*—"I attempt to do what I haven't done before."
4. *The Creative Zone*—"I attempt to think what I have never thought before."

ASSESS

To which zone do you naturally gravitate? Do you tend to live in the coasting zone, casually—even passively—doing as little as possible? Do you tend to stay in the comfort zone, avoiding risks? Do you connect with the challenge zone, where you try new things and willingly risk failure? Or do you try to stretch yourself the furthest by living in the creative zone, where you explore new ideas, seek out other perspectives, and cross bridges in your imagination long before you physically reach them?

(continued)

Look at the four zones and indicate what percentage of the time you spend in each. Make sure your answers total 100 percent.

The Coasting Zone—"I do as little as possible."	_____
The Comfort Zone—"I do what I have always done."	_____
The Challenge Zone—"I attempt to do what I haven't done before."	_____
The Creative Zone—"I attempt to think what I have never thought before."	_____

Total	100 %

The good news is that we have the ability to choose a zone different from our natural one. And I recommend the creative zone, because it is where we experience abundance and expand our potential. If you want to take your leadership to ever-higher levels, you need to make the leadershift from maintaining to creating and try to live in the creative zone.

UNLOCK THE MENTAL BLOCKS THAT KEEP YOU OUT OF THE CREATIVE ZONE

How can you make the shift from maintaining to creating? I believe you must start the process from the inside out. Begin by removing some of the mental blocks that cripple so many people's creative potential. Roger von Oech wrote extensively about many of them in his book *A Whack on the Side of the Head*.[1] I've included some of my favorites. Which of these phrases do you find yourself thinking or saying?

MENTAL BLOCK #1: "FIND THE RIGHT ANSWER"

It's wrong to believe there is only one right answer to any question. There are always other solutions. If we believe they are there and we're willing to look for them, we will find them.

MENTAL BLOCK #2: "THAT'S NOT LOGICAL"

Albert Einstein said, "Imagination is more important than knowledge. Knowledge is limited. Imagination encircles the world."[2] Imagination turns possibilities into reality. It's willing to take leaps that logic can't. While logic does have great value and you should keep it, you should intentionally add creativity.

MENTAL BLOCK #3: "FOLLOW THE RULES"

I've always loved this quote from Thomas Edison: "There ain't no rules around here! We are tryin' to accomplish some[thing]!"[3] Most revolutionary ideas have been disruptive violations of set rules.

MENTAL BLOCK #4: "AVOID AMBIGUITY"

Life is complex. It's messy. It's contradictory and paradoxical. Why in the world would we think that we should—or could—avoid ambiguity? There is never one fixed way to understand something—everything can be understood in more than one way.

MENTAL BLOCK #5: "FAILURE IS BAD"

Creative people don't avoid failure. They see it as a friend. They know that if they are to experiment, innovate, and create, they will fail. They embrace risk.

MENTAL BLOCK #6: "DON'T BE FOOLISH"

To stand up is to stand out. You have to stick your neck out to put your head above the crowd. If others don't at first understand or accept you, so what? All the great dreamers looked foolish to someone. How you are perceived by others is less important than how effective you can be.

MENTAL BLOCK #7: "I'M NOT CREATIVE"

The mental block that most keeps us from being creative is believing we don't possess creativity. This self-perception is a barrier to talent, opportunity, and intelligence. But the truth is that everyone can learn to be creative. The only real block to creativity is our disbelief.

I love what blogger Hugh MacLeod said about this: "Everyone is born creative; everyone is given a box of crayons in kindergarten. Then when you hit puberty they take the crayons away and replace them with dry, uninspiring books on algebra, history, etc. Being suddenly hit years later with the 'creative bug' is just a wee voice telling you, 'I'd like my crayons back, please.'"[4]

CONSIDER

Which of the seven mental blocks hold you back? Why? What can you do to remove them from your thinking?

_____

_____

_____

_____

_____

_____

CREATIVE PRINCIPLES TO LEARN AND LIVE BY

If you want to shift from maintaining to creating in your life and leadership, then you need to take your crayons back. Here's how:

1. BUILD A CREATIVE CULTURE

If you lead a team, department, or organization, take responsibility for promoting creativity and building a creative culture. Several years ago, I read an article in *Forbes* that took tips from *Disciplined Dreaming* by Josh Linkner, and they provide great insight in how to make your organization's culture more creative.[5] I've interpreted his ideas, plus added a few of my own.

FUEL PASSION

Creativity requires time, tenacity, testing, options, U-turns, imagination, questions, failure, and change. All these things require a lot of energy. Passion provides the fuel.

CELEBRATE IDEAS

What gets celebrated gets done. If you reward ideas with money, praise, and opportunity, people will come to value ideas and work toward generating and sharing them.

FOSTER AUTONOMY

George S. Patton said, "Never tell people *how* to do things. Tell them *what* to do and they will surprise you with their ingenuity." What he was really talking about was allowing people to have enough autonomy to be creative. Micromanagement undermines creativity while freedom and flexibility foster it.

ENCOURAGE COURAGE

Creativity requires risk, and taking risks requires courage. As a leader, you need to model it and encourage it. As Daniel R. Denison of IMD Business School said, "There is always a premium on being able to deal with the unknown. People will venture there if they feel they'll be secure in doing it. It's the leader's job to create that sense of security."

MINIMIZE HIERARCHY

In creative environments, decisions are made closest to the problems. For that to happen, leaders need to minimize the number of layers between the top and the bottom. A few years ago, I read an article by Robert Kaplan in which he interviewed now-retired General Stanley McChrystal, who said, "Any complex task is best approached by flattening hierarchies. It gets everybody feeling like they're in the inner circle, so that they develop a sense of ownership."[6]

REDUCE RULES

Author Henry David Thoreau wrote, "Any fool can make a rule and every fool will mind it." Creativity gets stifled when everyone expends too much energy worrying about following rules. Too many rules cause idea anemia. General Douglas MacArthur said, "You are remembered for the rules you break." I like that idea.

FAIL FORWARD

I once saw a sign that said, "Company Motto: We make *new* mistakes." I love that. I'm a huge supporter of the idea of failing forward. So much that I wrote an entire book on the subject. If you fall down, you should learn from it, get up, and step forward. Any time you learn what doesn't work, you're a step closer to what does work.

START SMALL

Too often we want huge breakthroughs and innovations when we should be looking for small ones. If you want one great idea, look for a lot of good ideas. If you want to create something significant, build it in small increments. Do that consistently, and you make creative progress.

TAKE ACTION

Create a plan to make these ideas part of how your team works. You may want to begin by reducing hierarchy and celebrating (and rewarding) ideas.

_____

_____

_____

_____

_____

_____

_____

_____

The more you foster creativity in the environment you influence, the more you instill an abundance mind-set. That's why I call this leadershift the abundance shift. It's like poet Maya Angelou said, "You can't use up creativity. The more you use, the more you have. Sadly, too often creativity is smothered rather than nurtured. There has to be a climate in which new ways of thinking, perceiving, questioning are encouraged."[7] As a leader, you have the influence and an obligation to try to create that climate.

2. MAKE EVERYTHING BETTER

You've probably heard the expression, "It doesn't get any better than this." Well, I have news for you. It _can_ get better. Everything can get better. And as leaders, we should be catalysts for improvement. We need to champion the idea expressed by poet James Russell Lowell, who said, "Creativity is not the finding of a thing, but making something out of it after it is found."

Ask these questions to help spur this process: Can we take an idea to the next level? Can we target a message even more sharply? Can we make a client's experience even better? Can we add something to an event to make it spectacular? Is there anything important that the rest of the team didn't see because they were too far into the weeds and didn't have perspective? What can we do to go the extra mile? This phase is where great innovation often occurs and we are able to maximize ideas.

ASSESS

What is your mindset when it comes to getting work done? On a scale of 1 ("That's close enough.") to 10 ("Nothing's ever good enough."), how do you usually think? Circle the number that applies.

1   2   3   4   5   6   7   8   9   10

How does your mindset impact your ability to be creative and make things better? How could you improve?

_____

_____

_____

_____

_____

_____

_____

3. MAKE PLANS BUT LOOK FOR OPTIONS

No doubt good leaders use plans to get things done. But planning is not the end-all and be-all of leadership. Leaders who cling too inflexibly to a plan stifle creativity and miss opportunities. To be creative, leaders need to add options to their planning. I think of this as moving from Plan A to Option A.

More than two thousand years ago, Publilius Syrus wrote, "It is a bad plan that admits of no modifications." I believe what he really meant is that it's a bad *leader* whose plans don't allow modifications. Good leaders are flexible and their plans are fluid. They allow for creativity. They plan, but they look for options. And that's important. Options always present themselves soon after action is taken on a plan. If we don't open ourselves up to those options, we miss the chance to innovate, to create, and—sometimes—to win.

On his blog, author and speaker Steve Pavlina wrote about how good leaders look for options and make adjustments:

> Stephen Covey often used the expression, "Integrity in the moment of choice." What that means is that you should not follow your plans blindly without conscious awareness of your goals. For instance, let's say you're following your plans nicely—so far so good—and then an unforeseen opportunity arises. Do you stick to your original plan, thereby missing the opportunity, or do you stop and go after the opportunity, thereby throwing yourself off schedule? This is where you have to stop and reconnect with your goals to decide which is the better course. No plan should be followed blindly.[8]

The best leaders are flexible. As leadership author Warren Bennis said, "Adaptive capacity allows leaders to respond quickly and intelligently to constant change. It is the ability to identify and seize opportunities. It allows leaders to act and then evaluate results instead of attempting to collect and analyze all the data before acting."[9]

ASSESS

Are you a planner or an improviser? On a scale of 1 ("I make my plan and never deviate.") to 10 ("Plan? What's a plan?"), how would you score yourself? Circle the number that applies.

(continued)

1	2	3	4	5	6	7	8	9	10

How does your attitude impact your ability to get things done while still being creative? In which area do you most need to improve? How can you do that?

_____

_____

_____

_____

_____

_____

_____

4. PLACE HIGH VALUE ON IDEAS

Harvey Firestone, one of the most successful businessmen of the nineteenth and early twentieth centuries, said, "Capital isn't so important in business. Experience isn't so important. You can get both of these things. What is important is ideas. If you have ideas you have the main asset you need, and there isn't any limit to what you can do with your business and your life. They are any man's greatest asset—ideas." If you want to be creative, you must place high value on ideas and learn how to generate them.

CONSIDER

Where do you allow space for creativity in your team or department as you take on tasks? Review the steps below and write how you allow members of your team to inject creativity at each stage:

Task or Problem Identification: _____

_____

Information Gathering: _____

_____

Assessment: _____

Process Development: _____
_____

Assignment of Responsibilities: _____
_____

Process Implementation: _____
_____

In-Process Problem Solving: _____
_____

Post Implementation Assessment:
_____
_____
_____
_____

5. SEEK OUT AND LISTEN TO DIFFERENT VOICES

Creativity thrives when one subject is approached from many different perspectives. It short-circuits the kind of one-way thinking that interferes with better solutions. If we get into single-perspective thinking, we find ourselves in ruts. If we see things from a new perspective, we can be like the mechanic who told his customer, "I couldn't repair your brakes, so I just made the horn louder."

CREATIVITY THRIVES WHEN ONE SUBJECT IS APPROACHED FROM MANY DIFFERENT PERSPECTIVES.

Norman Vincent Peale said, "Ask the God who made you to keep remaking you." I do that. I try to remain teachable, and I listen to many different voices and perspectives to try to improve myself. That's why I always try to surround myself with the best and the brightest people I can find. I like nothing more than to bring together a group of leaders, young and old, new and experienced, and ask them for their perspectives on a question, problem, or project. I'm a firm believer in the T-E-A-M principle: Together Everyone Accomplishes More. I want others' assessments. And I love that word: *assessment*. It comes from the Latin *assidere*, which means "to sit beside." I want people willing to sit beside me, share their perspectives, give their insights, add their ideas to mine, and make all of us better.

From about the age of forty, I have greatly valued the help of my inner circle, the people closest to me in life and in business. These individuals compensate for my weaknesses, focus on today, and implement much of the work in my organizations. Most of these people have worked with me for many years, some for more than two decades. But over the last few years, I have intentionally cultivated another group that I call my outer circle. These people have fresh eyes and can speak to me from a different perspective. They enhance my strengths, help me focus on tomorrow, and give me creative ideas. The people in this group change frequently, based on time and opportunities. Together, both circles complement or empower each other and complete me.

CONSIDER

Do you have an inner circle? An outer circle? Who you allow to give you creative or critical input into your life? List the people you invite and allow to speak into your life, along with the primary contribution they make.

_____

_____

_____

_____

_____

_____

_____

_____

_____

6. LIVE ON THE OTHER SIDE OF "YES"

Recently I was casting vision to a large group of leaders. There was a great sense of anticipation as I shared the possibilities and opportunities that could be before us if we partnered together and joined hands to accomplish this vision. After that session, I met in the green room with the top leaders of that organization, continuing to discuss the possibilities of working together. One of those leaders, Larry Stockstill, interrupted the discussion and said, "John, the answer is yes. Count me in. Whatever this means, I am a 'yes.'" His response energized the room and everyone followed his positive lead.

After the meeting when Larry and I were together, I thanked him for his positive response. I was curious, so I asked what made him respond so boldly.

"I live on the other side of 'yes,'" Larry said, "That's where I find abundance and opportunity. It's where I become a better and bigger self. The opportunity of a lifetime must be seized within the lifetime of the opportunity. So I try to say 'yes' whenever I can."

How can you become more opportunistic and live on the other side of "yes"?

IMAGINE OPPORTUNITIES EVERYWHERE

Everything mankind has accomplished existed in someone's imagination before it became a reality. We create what we imagine, and imagination is one of the last remaining legal means you have to gain what feels like an unfair advantage over your competition. You can cultivate this imagination by:

- *Asking Questions:* Curious people are imaginative people, and questions are doorways to opportunity
- *Networking:* You are only a few people away from a wonderful opportunity. Right now, someone knows something you should know, and someone is doing something you should do.
- *Taking Action:* Action creates opportunities. The best opportunity is seldom behind the first door, but going through that first door will be essential to get to the other doors that present the better opportunities.

Opportunities are like rabbits. You get a couple and learn to handle them, and soon you have a dozen. An opportunity grasped and used produces another opportunity. The more successful you are, the more opportunities will be given to you.

PREPARE FOR OPPORTUNITIES

To be prepared for opportunity, you must produce results and make sure that you are the most qualified when the door opens. Are you working as hard as you can? Are you learning as much as you can? Are you connecting with others as often as you can? Are you building a team as well as you can? All these things make you ready and put you closer to the door when it opens.

ACTIVATE YOUR CURRENT OPPORTUNITIES

It's always easier to see opportunities we've missed, the ones behind us, than to see the ones in front of us now. To live on the other side of "yes," we need to focus on the current moment and activate whatever opportunity is presenting itself. We need to open the door before us, not lament the doors behind us that we missed. We must stay hungry, believe we will have opportunities, seize the small ones when we find them, and build upon them until we are ready for even bigger challenges.

Robert Lynch, president and CEO of Americans for the Arts, said, "Creativity is the most effective response to rapid change." Why? Because creativity always adds. Leadershifting from maintaining to creating allows you to lead people into the land of abundance and opportunity.

If you desire to be successful and to be the best leader you can possibly be, you cannot settle for the familiar. You cannot live in your comfort zone. Don't ever get comfortable. Make the shift to abundance. Get out on the edge. Break new ground. Seize opportunity. Get creative.

CONSIDER

What can you do to make the most of your opportunities and live on the other side of yes? Write how you will improve in the following areas:

Imagine and Identify Opportunities:

_____

_____

_____

_____

Prepare for Opportunities:

_____

_____

_____

_____

Activate Current Opportunities:

_____

_____

_____

_____

MAINTAINING TO
CREATING

THE ABUNDANCE SHIFT

DISCUSSION QUESTIONS

1. Which gives you the greatest inner satisfaction: executing a perfect plan, rethinking an old plan, or creating a new plan from scratch? Why?

2. Which of the mental blocks listed in the lesson is the most difficult for you to overcome?

   - "Find the right answer."
   - "That's not logical."
   - "Follow the rules."
   - "Avoid ambiguity."
   - "Failure is bad."
   - "Don't be foolish."
   - "I'm not creative."

   Why does it challenge you? What could you do to improve in that area?

3. How do you find your best ideas? How do you record them so that you don't lose them? How do you decide which to implement?

4. How do you think risk and creativity are connected?

5. What is the greatest challenge to creating a creative culture on a team? What can you do to make yourself and your team more creative and innovative?

NOTES

LESSON SEVEN

LADDER CLIMBING TO
LADDER BUILDING

THE REPRODUCTION SHIFT

If I have seen farther than others, it is by standing on the shoulders of giants.

ISAAC NEWTON

I've always been a talker, from the time I was a child, through high school, in college, and into my career as a pastor. That trait, coupled with a desire to improve as a communicator and a degree of success in leadership, landed me some big opportunities to speak at a relatively young age. Sometimes I got to speak before large crowds alongside some amazing speakers.

When I started getting these great opportunities for speaking gigs, my excitement was always mixed with fear. My eagerness to get out and speak was often tempered by worry because of my lack of experience. I was glad for the exposure and the chance to teach new audiences, but I was also aware that I was in over my head. Early in my speaking career, at most events, I was at the bottom of the class.

I dealt with this by becoming the chief cheerleader of all the other speakers whenever I got invited to speak. I sat in the front row. I laughed at their stories. I wrote down all their insights. I stood and cheered as they walked offstage. And I stood in line to thank them for helping me after the event.

After the thrill of being part of such wonderful speaking teams started to wear off, I began to analyze my communication and my impact on my audiences. Here's what I discovered: after I was done speaking, there was lots of inspiration but not a lot of application. People who heard me speak were glad they came, but they weren't sure what to do with anything I said when they got home. I was encouraging everybody, but I wasn't helping anybody.

Time to Make a Change

It took me a while to figure out my problem, but after asking experienced communicators questions and listening to their responses, I realized what was wrong. My focus was totally on myself. The experience was more about me than the people I was there to help. My subject matter, my stories, my points, my thoughts, my delivery—it was all for me. After I spoke, the questions I was asking myself afterward were, *How did I do? Did they like me? Did they like what I said? Did they clap for me? Were they impressed by my talent? Do they admire me?*

When I realized what I had been doing, I felt exposed and saw the error of my ways. And I knew that I had to make a shift. My speaking had to change. So did my attitude. I needed to focus on others and on adding value to them when I spoke.

I took some time to reflect. I wondered how I could make the changes needed in this area. So I wrote something to help me. This is what I wrote:

- It's not about me—it's about them.
- Success is not a standing ovation—it's people walking out with a game plan.
- My talk is not to help me look good—it's to help them get good.
- If they can't relate to what I want to say—I shouldn't say it.
- If they can't apply what I say to their lives—I shouldn't say it.
- When I'm done, don't expect them to give me a hand—invite them to come shake my hand.
- When they walk away, hope that they say, "His name is John and he's my friend."

Eventually, this shift started to bleed into my leadership, where it wasn't ever supposed to be about me. Leadership should always be about others.

Before this, I was a ladder climber. Nearly everything I did was motivated by the question, "How high can I go?" But making this shift helped me to realize that there was more to life than getting to the top. Instead of just trying to be successful personally, I could help others. And over the years, I realized that there were a series of shifts I could make, and they came in stages.

1. *Ladder Climbing*—"How high can I go?"
2. *Ladder Holding*—"How high will others go with a little help?"
3. *Ladder Extending*—"How high will others go with a lot of help?"
4. *Ladder Building*—"Can I help them build their own ladder?"

This leadershift is about changing from being a personal producer to an equipper of others. It's a shift that takes your leadership math from addition to multiplication. It takes you from the solitary climb to the top of your ladder, where you might enjoy the view and wave to the people down below, to watching many people climb to the top of their own ladders, and you all enjoy the view from the top together.

LADDER STAGES

I want to explain the four stages that I went through to help you make this shift in your leadership:

1. LADDER CLIMBING—"HOW HIGH CAN I GO?"

Wanting to climb the ladder yourself isn't a bad thing, because credibility in leadership is often built on personal success. No one wants to follow a leader who cannot succeed. People want to be on a team only if they know they have a chance to win. So the first step in leadership is not leading others. It's leading yourself; it's showing you are capable of climbing the ladder yourself.

Speaker Glen Turner once told me, "The hardest challenge of getting to the top of the ladder was getting through the crowd at the bottom." Being able to climb the ladder yourself is the first step in separating yourself from the rest of the crowd. If you need help in figuring out how to do that, ask yourself these three questions:

> THE HARDEST CHALLENGE OF GETTING TO THE TOP OF THE LADDER
> WAS GETTING THROUGH THE CROWD AT THE BOTTOM.
>
> GLEN TURNER

WHAT ARE MY STRENGTHS?

Success comes from building upon your strengths and making the most of them, not from bringing your weaknesses up to par. For example, three of my top strengths are strategy, activation, and Woo (from StrengthsFinder).[1] Where am I weak? I don't do well with tasks related to administration or maintenance. And I'm absolutely terrible when it comes to anything technical. Any time or energy spent in these areas would be a total waste. Know what your strengths are and start developing them.

CONSIDER

What are your top three to five strengths?

_____

_____

_____

_____

_____

_____

WHAT ARE MY OPPORTUNITIES?

I believe everyone has opportunities. I do, and I'm convinced you do. The opportunities you receive may not be as big as you want. They may not be the kind that you want. But they are opportunities. What should you do with them? Apply your strengths to them and make the most of them. The meeting of your strengths with an opportunity is where you get the chance to start climbing the ladder. Make the most of it. Even if it's not the perfect opportunity—and trust me, it won't be, because there is no such thing—you can start the climb. Once you climb up out of the crowd, you'll discover other, better opportunities.

CONSIDER

What are your best opportunities that fit your strengths?

_____

_____

_____

_____

_____

_____

Am I Taking Steps Every Day?

When you seize an opportunity and apply your strengths to it, you still have to do the work. If you can't answer yes to the question of whether you're taking steps every day, you won't succeed, and you'll have to forget about taking the next step toward becoming a ladder builder.

CONSIDER

What steps are you taking every day to maximize at least one of those opportunities? If you're not currently taking steps, what steps *could* you be taking? Write them down, and commit yourself to following through with them consistently.

_____

_____

_____

_____

_____

How high do you need to climb? My answer is that you need to get to the top 10 percent. That's the magic number. That's where you become set apart from all the rest in the areas of money, influence, opportunity, and relationships. That's where the quality of people who want to be on your team changes drastically. So as you work to climb the ladder yourself, one of the things you need to ask yourself is whether you can get to that top 10 percent. If you can, then you will be able to start holding the ladder for others.

As you climb the ladder of success, here's some advice for making sure you're doing it as effectively as possible:

- Make sure your ladder is on a firm foundation of integrity and strong character.
- Make sure your ladder is leaning against the right "building" for your purpose.
- Never step on other people while climbing up.
- Don't skip any rungs of the ladder.
- Step back down occasionally to rest, reflect, and gain perspective.
- Don't step on anyone while descending either.
- Each time you start to climb back up, make sure you improve.
- Always value the people who are holding the ladder for you.

The better you are at climbing the ladder yourself, the more you will have to give others when you move on to the next phases.

2. LADDER HOLDING—"HOW HIGH WILL OTHERS GO WITH A LITTLE HELP?"

Kevin Myers, the leader of 12Stone Church, said, "Leaders should want far more *for* their people than *from* their people." I talked a little about that in Lesson 1 on shifting from soloist to conductor. When you want more for others and you're willing to give them some help, it's like holding the ladder for another person, giving them a secure base, empowering them to take moderate risks, and allowing them to climb higher.

I've benefited from many people who were willing to hold the ladder for me as I climbed, especially when I was younger. Their initial support was key to my success. They made me better. And their help inspired me to want to help others. If you've been successful, you're ready to begin helping others by holding the ladder for them. Here are the things you need to know to get started:

Ladder Holding Begins with a Serving Attitude

Ralph Waldo Emerson said, "Our chief want in life is somebody who shall make us do what we can." Adopting a serving attitude so that we will hold the ladder for others helps us to do what we can. Plus, living out an attitude of service sets a good example to the team and is a visual reminder of the importance of servanthood. When you show the people you work with that you are willing and able to serve, then they will be willing and able to serve.

Ladder Holding Requires Availability

To become a ladder holder, you must be open to people and willing to give of yourself. When someone asks a question, you must be willing to answer. If you're asked for an opinion, you need to be willing to talk. When people want your ideas, you need to jump in. If they want your endorsement, give it. Ladder holding is one leader helping another leader. When you engage with young leaders, value them, believe in them, encourage them, and give resources to them. Make yourself available to them.

Ladder Holding Attracts People Who Want to Climb

The greatest way to raise up good leaders is to recruit people with good leadership potential. How do you attract those kinds of individuals? Develop a reputation for investing in others. Young, talented people who desire to achieve will begin seeking you out if you become known for giving others a leg up.

Ladder Holding Is a Pre-Qualifier for Discovering a Person's Potential

How do you gauge others' ability to grow? How do you determine whether they can become good or even great leaders? By watching how they perform when given opportunities. By holding the ladder and offering them the chance to climb, you find out whether they take the steps they can and how quickly and easily they perform. You get a sense of their ability and desire. And that gives you insight into their eventual potential.

Ladder Holding Over Time Multiplies Effectiveness

Business magnate and philanthropist Andrew Carnegie said, "It marks a big step in your development when you come to realize that other people can help you do a better job than you could do alone." I've discovered that helping others helps me. Over the years, being a ladder holder has given me a huge ROI (return on investment).

* * *

My friend Chris Hodges said, "A dream is a compelling vision you see in your heart that is too big to accomplish without the help of others." When you start holding the ladder for others, you enlist their help. To take them to an even higher level, you need to do more.

CONSIDER

As you lead your team, do you want more *from* them or *for* them? Take a moment to write the names of each team member along with what you want from them and want for them. You will hold the ladder only for those you want to help.

Team Member	Want from Them	Want for Them

3. LADDER EXTENDING—"HOW HIGH WILL OTHERS GO WITH A LOT OF HELP?"
The next step in the process is to extend the ladder for others. When you do that, you empower them to climb higher and go to entirely new levels. How do you do that? By intentionally and strategically mentoring them.

Over the years I've sought out a lot of mentors who have extended the ladder for me. I've also been a mentor to many leaders, so I know this territory pretty well. Whether you're in the stage of your leadership to be extending the ladder to others, or you're looking for someone to help you develop, here are the criteria for being a good mentor:

LADDER EXTENDERS ARE SUCCESSFUL

Who you learn from is as important as what you learn. Good mentors are successful. Since the word *mentor* is both a verb, something you do, and a noun, something you are, a good mentor must exhibit ability in both areas. In the area of doing, this means they are productive. When it comes to being, good mentors possess strong character. If both components aren't there, don't consider asking them to mentor you.

SINCE THE WORD *MENTOR* IS BOTH A VERB, SOMETHING YOU DO, AND A NOUN, SOMETHING YOU ARE, A GOOD MENTOR MUST EXHIBIT ABILITY IN BOTH AREAS.

LADDER EXTENDERS ARE SPECIALISTS

A mentor ought to be very skilled in just a few areas. Often, people seek out a mentor to help them in all areas of their lives. That's not realistic. No one can help you with everything. Instead of looking for one mentor, seek out several for each key area in your life that you're working on.

That said, when you're first starting out and learning the basics, one solid leader may be a sufficient help to you. As you advance and become more specialized in your growth, your mentors will need to be more specialized.

LADDER EXTENDERS ARE MATURE

The whole idea of working with a mentor implies that the person is ahead of you. He or she is bigger, faster, more knowledgeable, and more experienced. It means the person possesses maturity. Why is maturity essential in a mentor's life? Because we teach what we know, but we reproduce who we are.

LADDER EXTENDERS ARE PRACTICED IN THE ART OF ASKING GREAT QUESTIONS

Good mentors don't jump to conclusions. They ask questions and explore ideas to unlock doors that would otherwise remain locked. I emphasize this because I have not always been good at asking questions. I used to be very quick with answers and had to slow down to become a better listener.

A lot of leaders are too quick to give direction when what they need to do is ask questions. If you're in a place to start extending the ladder for others, develop the ability to ask questions and carefully listen. And if you are working with a mentor and the person isn't asking you any questions, be aware that he or she may not be able to take you very far in the process.

LADDER EXTENDERS ARE HUMBLE

The mentoring relationship is at its best when both people meet and interact on common ground. This is especially important since the mentor is usually working from the position of greater strength, position, and experience. How is this common ground maintained? Through the humility of the mentor. If he or she maintains an openness to sharing failures, disappointments, and losses, the person being mentored benefits tremendously.

ASSESS

Are you ready to mentor others? Mark your answer beside each statement.

YES	NO	
❑	❑	I am successful in my career.
❑	❑	I have expertise as a specialist.
❑	❑	I possess maturity, I see the big picture, and I can keep a confidence.
❑	❑	I'm a good listener skilled at asking questions.
❑	❑	I possess humility and will treat those I mentor as equals.

4. LADDER BUILDING—"CAN I HELP THEM BUILD THEIR OWN LADDER?"

Once you've climbed the ladder of success yourself, begun to hold it for others, and then learned how to extend it for emerging leaders by mentoring them, there's still another level you can go to as a developer of people. You can become a ladder builder. One of the best ladder-building leaders I know is Sam Chand. He has written several books that contain the word *ladder* in the title: *Who's*

Holding Your Ladder?, *What's Shaking Your Ladder?*, and *Who Moved Your Ladder?* Sam's license plate is LDDRMAN, and he was my inspiration for the title of this lesson.

Ladder building is all about giving another leader the permission, equipment, and empowerment to create their own ladder. As a leader, if you surround yourself with excellent people with high potential, there will be a time when you should allow them to build their own ladders. That's the time when you release them to lead on their own.

ASSESS

To lay the groundwork for becoming a ladder builder, start by asking yourself some questions:

YES	NO	
☐	☐	Do I develop leaders to benefit others, not just for myself and my team?
☐	☐	Do I relinquish control and give other leaders the freedom to be themselves and develop their own process?
☐	☐	Am I happy for a leader I help to move on without me or to enlist other mentors?
☐	☐	Am I willing to help other leaders build their own ladders and then genuinely root for them?
☐	☐	Am I willing to keep helping many leaders build their own ladders without expecting to receive any credit?

If you can answer yes to these questions, and you've climbed up the ladder enough yourself to have earned credibility, then you are ready to start your journey to becoming a ladder builder. If you're not ready, keep building your success and holding the ladder for others while working to shift your attitude to the place you can answer yes to these questions. Then start helping others and mentoring them. And when you see an opportunity to encourage others to build their own ladders, don't hesitate to give them a hand.

QUESTIONS TO ASK BEFORE YOU MENTOR SOMEONE

Andy Stanley often says, "Do for one what you wish you could do for many." That's great advice. And when it comes to investing in and helping someone by holding, extending, and building his or her ladder, it's important who you choose as that one. Your time is limited, and if you can spend time with only one person, it has to be the right one. With that in mind, ask the following questions about anyone you are considering helping:

1. IS THIS PERSON HUNGRY TO LEARN?

Author Napoleon Hill said, "Strong, deeply rooted desire is the starting point of all achievement."[2] Much of what people accomplish in their lives is based more on how much they want it than on how easy it was to get. Hope says, "There must be a way," while hunger says, "I will make a way." People with hope are many; people with hunger are few. I want to mentor one of the few. If you have to talk the person into being helped or convince him or her to follow through on your advice, that may not be someone you should be investing in. As poet Rudyard Kipling said, "If you don't get what you want it is either a sign that you did not seriously want it, or that you tried to bargain over the price."

2. WHAT IS THIS PERSON'S CAPACITY?

Hunger is easy to evaluate. Capacity is much more difficult. When I'm considering whether to mentor someone, I use the seven capacities that I wrote about in my book *No Limits* to evaluate him or her:

1. *Energy Capacity*—their ability to push on physically
2. *Emotional Capacity*—their ability to manage emotions
3. *Thinking Capacity*—their ability to think effectively
4. *People Capacity*—their ability to build relationships
5. *Creative Capacity*—their ability to see options and find answers
6. *Production Capacity*—their ability to accomplish results
7. *Leadership Capacity*—their ability to lift and lead others

I want anyone I mentor to show plenty of potential to grow in all seven areas. As David Salyers of Chick-fil-A said, "The mentor pours into the student knowing that as that person grows the return will be greater than the investment." People cannot show a great return if they don't have adequate capacity.

3. ARE THIS PERSON'S VALUES COMPATIBLE WITH MINE?

Shared values give you a track to run on with someone you intend to mentor. They provide a very important common ground and philosophical foundation. When I prepare to mentor people, I want to know that they . . .

- *Add Value to People*—They must be givers who want to help others, as I do.
- *Value Personal Growth*—They must demonstrate a lifestyle of learning.
- *Lead by Example*—They understand that follow me are the best words a leader can say to a follower.
- *Exceed Expectations*—They stand out and receive 80 percent of life's ROI.
- *Live Intentionally*—They know that everything worthwhile is uphill, and they climb intentionally every day.

Only if we share these common values will I invest time in them. Do you know what your values are? Identify them clearly so that you know whether or not you should invest in a potential candidate.

4. IS THIS INDIVIDUAL A LEADER?

Because my particular calling is to add value to leaders who multiply value to others, I will not invest in a person who is not a leader. I know that may sound very narrow, but it's focused and strategic. I discovered that when I mentor a leader, the ROI is much greater than if I pour myself into a follower. With a leader, I truly can do for one what I wish I could do for many, because that leader will influence many. With followers, that is not necessarily true.

CONSIDER

Before you mentor someone, be sure you can answer yes to these four questions:

YES	NO	
☐	☐	Is this person hungry to learn?
☐	☐	Does this person have the capacity to grow?
☐	☐	Are this person's values compatible with mine?
☐	☐	Is this individual a leader?

What do leaders need from a mentor? I like what Tim Elmore, the founder and president of Growing Leaders, says about this. Tim is one of the emerging leaders I helped more than thirty years ago. First I helped hold his ladder, then extend it. And more than twenty years ago, I helped him build his own ladder and cheered him on. He speaks extensively on mentoring and has written about it too. Some of the things Tim says a successful mentor gives to the person being mentored are: handles, laboratories, road maps, roots, and wings.[3] Let me explain:

HANDLES

Good mentors distill truths from complexity and divide the information into bite-sized principles that others can apply. All good mentors can put life lessons into a nutshell that is transferable. Are you willing to do the homework necessary to do that?

LABORATORIES

Good mentors provide a safe place where learners can practice the principles they're learning. Are you willing to create such a safe environment where people you're developing can take risks?

ROAD MAPS

Good mentors give learners direction for life and provide roadmaps of options for how to proceed to their destination. Are you willing to follow through with a good game plan for the people you mentor?

ROOTS

Good mentors provide learners with a solid relational foundation. Giving stability and security makes it possible for other people to grow and flourish. Are you willing to extend love and acceptance to the people you mentor and hang in there with them when they face difficulties?

WINGS

Good mentors help people to see new horizons and fly to places beyond where they imagined they could go. This is true empowerment. Are you willing to celebrate when people you mentor fly higher or farther than you have?

WHYS

I want to add one more quality to Tim's list. One of the most important things you can do for potential leaders is to help them see the big picture by teaching them the *why*s. This gives them context. It reveals to them the thinking and reasons behind your decisions. It teaches them decision-making. If you want learners to follow directions, you only need to provide the *what*. If you want them to lead others and give directions, they must also have the *why*. Are you willing to take the time and trouble to give them the *why* behind every *what*?

ACTION PLAN

Pick a leader with potential to mentor. Once you're sure he or she meets the four criteria above, write out an action plan for this person. Be sure to include handles, laboratories, road maps, roots, wings, and whys.

_____

_____

_____

_____

_____

_____

_____

_____

**IF YOU WANT LEARNERS TO FOLLOW DIRECTIONS,
YOU ONLY NEED TO PROVIDE THE *WHAT*. IF YOU WANT THEM TO LEAD OTHERS
AND GIVE DIRECTIONS, THEY MUST ALSO HAVE THE *WHY*.**

The bottom line is that leaders who shift from ladder climber to ladder builder help new leaders stretch to their potential. That's what I hope to do for the rest of my life and to leave as my legacy. And I invite you to do the same. You'll never regret investing in another leader who makes a positive difference in this world. It's the best way to extend your influence and achieve significance.

LADDER CLIMBING TO
LADDER BUILDING

THE REPRODUCTION SHIFT

DISCUSSION QUESTIONS

1. Where have you focused most of your time and energy in your career?

   - Climbing the Ladder of Success
   - Holding the Ladder for Others
   - Extending the Ladder for Others
   - Building Ladders for Others

2. Do you believe a leader needs to progress from holding to extending to building ladders? Or can a leader simply jump from climbing the ladder to building ladders for others? Explain your answer.

3. What experience do you have with being mentored? How was it? How did it benefit you? What didn't you like about it?

4. What experience do you have being a mentor to others? How did that go? What did you do well? What do you wish you would have done better? Was the time you put in worth the effort? Explain.

5. What impact would focusing on ladder building would have on you personally and professionally? What impact would it have on your leadership? What step in that direction would you be willing to commit to immediately?

NOTES

LESSON EIGHT

DIRECTING TO
CONNECTING

THE COMMUNICATION SHIFT

You don't lead by hitting people over the head—that's assault, not leadership.

DWIGHT D. EISENHOWER

All of the leadershifts in my life have not occurred in the same way or on the same timetable. Some have occurred gradually while others were almost instantaneous. Many were prompted by my leadership intuition, which has often been the catalyst for the changes I made. But some, like the communication shift from directing to connecting, went against my natural grain. This was a shift in the opposite direction of my experience, and it required time to develop.

I grew up in a home where directing was the practiced style of communication and leadership. My college theological training in communication and leadership reinforced this a methodology. In leadership, the authority in our ecclesiastical world was top-down. So I came from an upbringing and training that emphasized directing. On top of all this, my temperament is choleric, which means I love to be in charge and tell others what to do. I know where I want to go, and I'm not shy about saying how we should get there. If you have a question, I've got an answer. If you're not sure about what you want to do, I can give you a plan for your life.

Directing others was a very natural leadership style for me. But what's natural for me is not necessarily what's best for others. Nobody wants to be bossed around. Many times I could sense that people were following me only because they had to, not because they wanted to. Even those who wanted to follow me didn't always buy into the vision and direction I was communicating as strongly as I had hoped. Intuitively, I began to understand that I needed to move away from directing. I no longer wanted to be a "leadership cop" standing at the intersection of my organization and directing traffic all the time. But at the same time, I didn't know what else to do. What better way was there to lead people?

WELCOME TO A NEW PARADIGM

Two experiences functioned as catalysts to help me reshape my communication and leadership style. The first occurred in 1988. That was the year I hired Bobb Biehl as a consultant. This was my first experience hiring a business consultant, and it was before I had developed much experience as a ladder builder, so the way Bobb started the process took me totally by surprise. We spent two days together and the entire first day Bobb asked me questions. The entire day! He'd ask a question, I'd answer, and he'd ask follow-up questions based on my answers. He worked with flip charts, writing the questions and the answers. At the end of the day, every wall in my office was covered with sheets of paper containing everything we had talked about. I was exhausted yet fulfilled. In those hours Bobb had drawn out my innermost thoughts, hopes, and aspirations in a way that never had been done before. With each question, he had peeled away another layer, revealing the depth of my thinking and feelings. It was exhilarating.

I learned an important lesson from that. Bobb had to *find* me—who I was, where I was, where I had been, where I hoped to go—before he could *lead* me. That opened my eyes to a better way of leading, and the discovery became the foundation of my practice of connecting with others. From then on, I started working to find people by asking questions before trying to lead them.

The second experience that impacted me greatly occurred in 2003. I was invited to attend a basketball game of the University of Tennessee Lady Volunteers coached by the great Pat Summitt. I attended their pregame and sat right behind the bench. At halftime, I was able to go into the locker room and observe how Pat coached the team.

When we got to the locker room, Pat and the other coaches huddled together away from the players, while the players immediately sat in a semicircle around a whiteboard that had three questions written on it: (1) What did we do right in the first half? (2) What did we do wrong? (3) What do we need to change?

For five minutes, the players discussed their answers to those three questions while one player wrote down their responses. I sat behind the players and watched. I was fascinated. Then Pat walked over to the marker board and looked at the answers. She made a couple of comments related to what they had written, and then she sent the players back out on the floor to warm up for the second half.

After the game I asked Pat about it, and her answer was stunning.

"John, too many leaders lead by assumption," she said. "They assume they know where their people are. That halftime exercise lets me find my players so I can lead them. That can only be done by asking questions and listening to their answers."

That was a huge "aha" moment for me and was the second bookend in my leadershift from directing to connecting. I was determined from that moment forward to use connecting as the basis for my leadership and communication style.

CONSIDER

Take a moment and look at the contrast between these two styles. On each line, mark the box that represents your natural style.

DIRECTING	CONNECTING
☐ Authoritative	☐ Collaborative
☐ Talking	☐ Listening
☐ Top Down	☐ Side by Side
☐ Enlisting	☐ Empowering
☐ Assuming	☐ Understanding
☐ Gives Answers	☐ Asks Questions
☐ My Agenda	☐ Your Agenda

The goal of connecting is to find common ground with the leader initiating. This is the place where . . .

- both people meet;
- both people are valued;
- both people share;
- both people listen and learn;
- both people adjust;
- both people settle on a game plan;
- both people take ownership of the game plan; and
- both people move together to higher ground.

Learning to connect is one of the most important things you can do in life.

MAKE THE LEADERSHIFT TO CONNECTING

If you want to become the best leader you're capable of being, you must learn to connect with people. To do that, you must find ways to overcome the challenges of connecting and finding common ground. This can often be a difficult process, especially with a varied team. Here are the seven things I have found to be most important to a leader who wants to connect with others:

1. HUMILITY—LET PEOPLE KNOW YOU NEED THEM

Humility is essential in connecting with people. It took me a while to learn this. In my younger years, I would ask God to help me be successful, but secretly I hoped that people would think I did it all myself. I possessed more human frailty than humility. To help me, God gave me a dream bigger than myself. It was so intimidating that I had only two choices: give up or get help. I chose to ask for help, which at first felt very humbling. But I quickly discovered how much I needed other people. And as a result, my leadership actually got better, not worse.

> GOD GAVE ME A DREAM BIGGER THAN MYSELF. IT WAS SO INTIMIDATING THAT I HAD ONLY TWO CHOICES: GIVE UP OR GET HELP.

Good leaders are aware that they need other people, and they let them know that. There really is no downside. It keeps the leader's ego in check, it connects the leader and the people on the team, it draws team members into the center, and it better enables them to fulfill the vison. So, if you want to be a connector, acknowledge your shortcomings and need for others and be willing to ask for help.

CONSIDER

How often do you tell the people on your team that you need them and are grateful for their contribution? How often do you admit where you lack ability and thank them for theirs?

_____

_____

_____

_____

_____

_____

_____

2. CURIOSITY—ASK PEOPLE QUESTIONS

I'm known for asking questions. Whether I'm at dinner with friends, taking my grandchildren on a trip, or leading a business meeting, people know I'll be asking them questions. But I got my start as a questioner by asking myself questions. One of the things that stirred me to start asking myself better questions was Bob Buford's book *Halftime*. He had an important question for someone who is middle-aged, which I was at the time I first read the book more than twenty years ago. His question: "What kind of second half are you going to live?" Buford wrote:

You will not get very far in your second half without knowing your life mission. Can yours be stated in a sentence or two? A good way to begin formulating one is with some questions (and nakedly honest answers).

What is your passion? What have you achieved? What have you done uncommonly well? How are you wired? Where do you belong? What are the "shoulds" that have trailed you during the first half? These and other questions like them will direct you toward the self your heart longs for; they will help you discover the task for which you were especially made.[1]

These questions helped me at mid-life to set myself up for potentially a good second half.

Today I'm in my seventies, and I haven't stopped asking questions. I'm still curious, and I want to remain that way. Why? Because without asking questions, I can easily become comfortable, stagnant. Entropy can easily set in. I would start to accept the status quo without asking if there were a better way. I would fail to recognize opportunities.

Too many leaders don't ask enough questions—of themselves or others. This happens for a variety of reasons:

- They assume they have the answers.
- They value what *they* think more than what *others* think.
- They prioritize directing others over understanding others.
- They don't recognize the need to find common ground.
- They don't understand that questions help to manage expectations.

I want to take a moment to address this final point. As leaders, we must manage expectations all the time. We have to deal with expectations we have for ourselves, expectations we have for others, and expectations others have for us. Any time our expectations or those of others don't align with what's actually happening, there are problems. In fact, I believe that disappointment is the gap between expectations and reality. How do we close that gap? By asking questions so that we can adjust our expectations. Knowing the expectations I have of myself makes me more self-aware, which paves the way for me to improve myself and become better. Knowing the expectations I have of others makes me better able to communicate with people and face reality. And knowing the expectations others have of me makes me better able to lead them. All of these connections are made when we use questions to build bridges with others.

CONSIDER

How often do you ask questions? Do you assume you have all the answers or have better answers than your team members? How can you become better at asking questions?

_____

_____

_____

_____

_____

_____

_____

_____

_____

3. EFFORT—GO OUT OF YOUR WAY TO CONNECT WITH PEOPLE

Oprah Winfrey said, "The big secret in life is that there is no big secret. Whatever your goal, you can get there if you are willing to work." That is certainly true in connecting with people—you have to make the effort.

My grandson, John, started taking golf lessons when he was twelve. After months of lessons, it finally became time for him to play on a golf course, and I wanted to be the one to take him. Before we began I said, "John, I want you to try to get a par on one of the holes. If you are able to get on the green and putt for par, I'll take a video of you taking the shot and dropping the ball into the hole. That way we can show it to the family."

For two days, we played golf and worked on getting John his first par on a golf course. Every time he putted for a par, I pulled out my phone and videoed him. Four different times, he got on the green and had a chance to putt for par and missed it. But late on the second day on the sixteenth hole, John attempted his par putt and rolled the ball into the cup. And I had it on video! The first par he ever made.

We celebrated on the green, and then I immediately shared the video with the rest of the family right then and there. I also got a picture of John holding up his scorecard, proudly showing off his par, with his arm around me.

Now, why did I do that when it was so much work? Well, first of all, it was fun. But more importantly, I wanted to make a meaningful memory with my grandson. It's something both of us will always remember. And it created a special connection between us—one that will last well beyond our time on the golf course.

Every relational connection starts with the decision to make the effort to connect. It ends with what I call the mirror test: Can you look into the mirror and say to yourself that you did your best? If so, you have passed the test. As my friend Art Williams said, "All you can do is all you can do, but all you can do is enough."

ALL YOU CAN DO IS ALL YOU CAN DO, BUT ALL YOU CAN DO IS ENOUGH.

ART WILLIAMS

If you care about people, you will be capable of coming up with ways to create connecting experiences with others. But it will take effort. And it will take even *more* effort to follow through on those ideas. But if you don't, you're not really doing all you can to connect—or to become the best leader you can be.

CONSIDER

How can you go out of your way to connect with members of your team? Write the names of each team member along with an idea for a way to connect.

_____

_____

_____

_____

_____

_____

_____

_____

4. Trustworthiness—Be Someone Others Can Count On

People do not connect with someone they don't trust. They connect with someone they can count on. Author and speaker Simon Sinek addressed this issue when he said, "People don't buy what you do, they buy why you do it." The *why* deals with motives. Those motives come from the heart and play out as trustworthiness if the motives are good and right.

As a leader, I know I have to keep my motives right. If my primary motivation is to add value to people and help them, then all is good. If not, I'll get off track. And I'm continually aware that to remain trustworthy in the eyes of others, I have to work at being continually successful in three areas:

1. Integrity in my life
2. Consistency in my actions
3. Competence in my work

When I do these things well, I become more trustworthy and am able to connect with people—and build the relationship. When I fail in one or more of these, I lose trust and have to work to regain the trust I've lost. Because I'm only human, I do fail sometimes. How do I regain lost trust? By following this process:

- I fully acknowledge what I have done wrong.
- I explain exactly what I am going to do to try to make things right.
- I give them an opportunity to share their perspective and add anything to what I shared with them.
- I do the work to fix the problem.
- I follow up with them to confirm that the problem was fixed to their satisfaction.

The bottom line is that I do what I can to make it right. And trust me: I've had to do this too many times to count. But it works. And it's always amazing to me how forgiving people are when I follow this process with them. What's even more amazing is how often the relationship is strengthened and improved. It's often even better than it was before. I think there is a valuable lesson from this about trustworthiness. We often lose trust and connection with one another not because of an occasional failing, but because we neglect to take the right steps afterward to restore the relationship. Don't allow that to happen to you. Make the effort to be trustworthy, and when you fail, do what's in your power to make things right.

CONSIDER

Where have you broken trust with someone in your life? Commit to addressing the wrong you did. Prepare by making notes here:

What I did wrong: _____
_____
_____

How I'm going to try to make it right: _____
_____
_____

When I am going to talk to them and hear their side: _____
_____
_____

When I will work to fix the problem: _____
_____
_____

When I will follow up with them: _____
_____
_____

5. GENEROSITY—GIVE FIRST, GIVE CONTINUALLY

Albert Einstein said, "A person first starts to live when he can live outside of himself." It could also be said that a person starts to give when he lives outside himself. And giving is a good way to connect with others.

A PERSON FIRST STARTS TO LIVE WHEN HE CAN LIVE OUTSIDE OF HIMSELF.

ALBERT EINSTEIN

I have never known a stingy person with a scarcity mind-set who was able to connect well with other people. They are too often self-driven and make decisions based on self-preservation. As theologian Henri Nouwen said, "When we refrain from giving, with a scarcity mentality, the little we have will become less. When we give generously, with an abundance mentality, what we give away will multiply."

A few years ago I came across a transcript of the commencement address given by author Stephen King to the 2001 graduating class of Vassar College. As you might expect, it's written eloquently. In his address, he talked about money and generosity:

We come in naked and broke. We may be dressed when we go out, but we're just as broke. Warren Buffett? Going to go out broke. Bill Gates? Going to go out broke. President Ferguson? Going to go out broke. Steve King? Broke. You guys? Broke. Not a crying dime between you. And how long in between? How long have you got to be in the chips? . . . Just the blink of an eye. . . .

Should you give away what you have? Of course you should. I want you to consider making your lives one long gift to others, and why not? All the other stuff you have is just on loan. All you want to get at the getting place, from the Maserati you may dream about to the retirement fund some guy will try to sell you on sooner or later—none of that is real. All that lasts in this world is what you pass on. The rest is smoke and mirrors. . . .

Giving isn't about the receiver or the gift but the giver. It's for the giver. One doesn't open one's wallet to improve the world, although it's nice when that happens. One opens one's wallet to improve one's self. I give because it's the only concrete way I have of saying I'm glad to be alive and that I can earn my daily bread doing what I love. I hope you will be similarly grateful to be alive and that you will also be glad to do whatever it is you wind up doing. . . .

So I ask you to begin the next great phase of your life by giving, and to continue as you begin. I think you'll find that in the end you get far more than you ever had and do more good than you ever dreamed.[2]

Generosity makes you a better person, it helps you to become a better leader, and it paves the way for you to connect with other people. If you're not already someone who gives first and gives continually, then I encourage you to try it.

CONSIDER

In what areas of your life are you a giver? What do you give? How often do you give? What could you start doing now to become more generous?

_____

_____

_____

_____

_____

_____

6. LISTENING—OPEN THE BEST DOOR TO CONNECTING WITH PEOPLE

I once read a story about a tennis pro who was giving a lesson to a new student. After watching the student take several swings at the tennis ball, the instructor began to suggest ways the man might improve his stroke. But every time the instructor made a suggestion, the student interrupted him with his own diagnosis of the problem and how he might fix it.

After being interrupted yet again, the pro simply nodded in agreement and let the player continue on his own.

When the lesson was over, a woman—who observed the lesson, was familiar with the pro, and had seen the whole thing—asked, "Why did you go along with that arrogant man's stupid suggestions?"

The old pro smiled and answered, "I learned a long time ago that it's a sheer waste of time to try to sell answers to a person who only wants to buy echoes."

If you never listen, before long the people around you will stop talking to you, and you'll become isolated as a leader. If you *do* listen, not only will they tell you things you need to know but they will also connect with you because they see that you care and that you value what they have to say.

It took me a while to learn this myself. As a young leader I was like the tennis student who didn't listen. My highest priority was expressing my ideas and convincing others to buy into them, not listening to feedback or learning what others had to say. After a series of leadership misses, I recognized the problem in my unwillingness to make listening a priority, and I began shifting to do things differently. But it was hard fought. I struggled to change, but I eventually succeeded. Here's how I did it.

- I Made a List of the Negatives of Not Listening Well
- I Reminded Myself Daily to Listen Well
- I Stopped Interrupting
- I Started Asking Questions
- I Invited People to Hold Me Accountable for Listening

If you want to be a connecting leader, become a better listener. Invite others to hold you accountable. If you have the courage, meet with your team members, colleagues, friends, and family, and ask them how good a listener you are on a scale of one to ten. If your score is low, you might need to take the same steps I did.

CONSIDER

Talk to the three people on your team with whom you have the least smooth working relationship, and ask them these questions:

- Do you think it would improve our working relationship if I became a better listener?
- When should I listen more?
- How do you think that would help?

(continued)

Don't interrupt them or defend yourself. Take notes and thank them for their input. Then reflect on what that told you.

_____

_____

_____

_____

_____

_____

_____

_____

_____

_____

_____

_____

_____

7. ENCOURAGEMENT—GIVE PEOPLE OXYGEN FOR THEIR SOUL

As leaders, we must never underestimate the value of reminding others that we believe in them. If even the greatest of leaders need encouragement, then everyone does. That's why George M. Adams called encouragement oxygen for the soul.

When you interact with others as a leader, what is your mind-set? Is your intention to correct them or connect with them? Do you keep them down, or lift them up? You have that choice every day—with those you lead, with those who lead you, with your friends, family, and colleagues.

WHEN YOU INTERACT WITH OTHERS AS A LEADER, WHAT IS YOUR MIND-SET? IS YOUR INTENTION TO CORRECT THEM OR CONNECT WITH THEM?

If you're a fan of *The Lord of the Rings* books, and *The Hobbit*, you might be surprised that their author, J. R. R. Tolkien, required the encouragement of a friend and fellow writer to keep him going in the early stages of his work on those books. C. S. Lewis and Tolkien used to gather, along with a few other friends, in a group they called the Inklings. They met weekly to share what they were working on and to encourage one another. Tolkien credited Lewis as the person who kept him going when he felt discouraged. In an article about the two writers, Mark Moring said:

> Had it not been for Lewis, Tolkien wouldn't have written *The Lord of the Rings*. Tolkien wrote in a letter, "The unspeakable debt I owe him cannot be fathomed. For long, he was my only audience." Several times Tolkien really threw in the towel, and each time Lewis said, "Tollers, where's that next chapter? You can't give up now." Lewis was the only one who kept him going.[3]

Everyone in your life could use the encouragement that only you can give. At home, I've always tried to provide encouragement, first to my children and now also to my grandchildren. I also take the mind-set of an encourager onto the stage when I speak. As a communicator, I can either try to be a *sage on the stage* or a *guide by their side*. A sage looks down on others and tries to impress them with wisdom. A guide comes alongside, shares the journey, and encourages them to go the distance with him. I don't want to impress others; I want to connect with them and help them.

Billionaire investor and philanthropist Charles Schwab said, "I have yet to find the man, however great or exalted his station, who did not do better work and put forth greater effort under a spirit of approval than he would ever do under a spirit of criticism."[4] I believe most people are under-encouraged. You can correct that deficit by becoming an encouraging leader.

ACTION PLAN

Make a commitment to say one encouraging thing every day this week to each person on your team. Pay attention to how people respond and whether the work atmosphere changes.

Changing from directing to connecting is one of the most valuable shifts you will ever make as a leader. When you direct, it's like building a bridge to others, but the traffic only goes one way. When you connect, it's a two-way street. And because of that, everything improves. Not only are relationships better, but ideas improve because they're flowing in both directions. People work better together, and the team gets stronger. Problems get solved more quickly because communication is better, people know one another better, and they start pulling together. And the environment improves too.

Will it take time to build these connections? The answer is yes. But don't let that stop you. In the long run, you'll save time. Your team will get better. And so will you.

DIRECTING TO
CONNECTING

THE COMMUNICATION SHIFT

DISCUSSION QUESTIONS

1. Who is the best leader you ever worked for? How much directing and how much connecting did he or she do?

2. In what situations is directing more effective? In what situations is connecting more effective? Which is better for long-term team success?

3. How much does personality type affect whether a leader naturally directs or connects? What can someone who's not naturally a connector do to improve in this area?

4. How much of the ability to connect comes from internal factors, such as humility, attitude, and trustworthiness, and how much comes from practices, such as reaching out to people, asking questions, and listening? Explain your answer.

5. What is your greatest obstacle or hesitation about connecting with team members? What can you do to overcome it?

NOTES

LESSON NINE

TEAM UNIFORMITY TO
TEAM DIVERSITY

THE IMPROVEMENT SHIFT

Our differences can make a positive difference.

Of all the leadershifts I've made, this required the greatest leap. I say that because there is nothing diverse about my background. I grew up in Circleville, Ohio. It was in the middle of the country. The community was almost entirely white. And my family was lower middle class. There was nothing cutting-edge about the church I grew up in. We were conservative and old-fashioned. Even the theological and ministry training I received at the college in Circleville emphasized that Christians should separate themselves from the culture of society in some ways. We set ourselves apart and were comfortable spending all our time with people like ourselves.

My early days as a pastor were equally vanilla. The church I led was filled with farmers and their families. They were good-hearted, hardworking, salt-of-the-earth types of people. But they were not diverse or forward-looking. While I was at the church, NASA put the first man on the moon. The people in my church were not convinced that it had actually happened. Many believed it was a hoax that had been staged in the desert of the American West with trampolines placed underground and covered with sand. Really? Yes, really!

All the leaders in the church were old white men. They all seemed to be cut from the same cloth, adhering to the same rules, following the same model of leadership. They even looked like one another. As a pastor, I was expected to conform to the way other churches in our organization operated and follow all the same rules and guidelines everyone else did. As I already mentioned in Lesson 6 on the abundance shift, the emphasis was on tradition and conformity. When it was time for me to hire my first staff member, the advice I received was to try to find a "John Jr.": someone exactly like me. Their concept of progress was moving backward slowly, and their idea of innovation was *more of the same*.

GETTING OUTSIDE OF THE BUBBLE

The improvement shift from uniformity to diversity occurred slowly for me. The seeds were sown for it while I was still in college. It started because I was coaching a basketball team at a Catholic school. This was my first exposure to and long-term interaction with Catholics. At that time, I also met the first priest I ever got to know: Father Mike Elifritz. He was wonderful. After I was done coaching and I was getting ready to graduate from college, I had a lunch with Father Mike. I shared with him some of my apprehension about the next steps I would be taking in life. I'll never forget what he told me: "John, trust your future to God." Those words helped me to be more confident as I moved into the next phase of living.

Why were those words so significant? After all, I was a person of faith who was actually going into ministry! They resonated strongly with me because a Catholic was adding value to a Protestant. In my small sheltered world, that wasn't supposed to happen. Those two groups stayed on opposite sides of the line and were suspicious of one another. But his heart and support changed my thinking. It was catalytic for me and started to show me a bigger, more diverse world.

That occurred in 1969 and was the start of a long journey toward the appreciation of diversity that would take almost thirty years. Along the way, there were a lot of experiences that challenged my narrow, naïve thinking, and a lot of lessons that I learned. Hundreds of people different from me made a positive difference in my life. They . . .

- challenged my assumptions,
- changed my thinking,
- showed me better ways of doing things,

- helped me remove my prejudices,
- taught me to value everyone, and
- made me a better person.

Slowly I moved from valuing sameness to questioning its value. Diversity slowly marked me with this thought: people different from me could make a positive difference in me.

PEOPLE DIFFERENT FROM ME COULD MAKE A POSITIVE DIFFERENCE IN ME.

This shift, which started subtly and grew over time, culminated when I re-located myself and my companies to Atlanta, Georgia, in 1997. Atlanta is a city rich in African-American influence and history. That was new to me. I'd lived in small-town Ohio, rural Indiana, and sunny San Diego. I knew there was a gap between me and the African-American community and their experiences, and I wanted to close that gap.

To help me, I enlisted the assistance of my friend Sam Chand, the president emeritus of Beulah Heights University, a predominantly African-American insti-tution in Atlanta. Sam was born in India, but he was well-connected in our com-munity. He arranged lunches every other month for two years where I got to meet more than three hundred local leaders. Overall, their journey was different from mine. I asked a lot of questions and requested that people tell me their stories. I'm happy to say that I was able to connect with most of the people I met. They reshaped my attitude, challenged my thinking, and touched my soul. I became a better person because of these experiences, and I made many new friends.

THE ADVANTAGES OF TEAM DIVERSITY

I saw a definition of *team* in the *Harvard Business Review* that I really like: "A team is a small number of people with complementary skills who are committed to a common purpose, set of performance goals, and approach for which they hold themselves mutually accountable."[1] This definition assumes that there is a variety of skills. That implies diversity.

Our differences really can make a difference in our teams, our organizations, and our individual lives. Once we find common ground and commit to bringing the best out of people who are diverse, good things will begin to happen. This is what I am discovering now.

1. DIVERSE TEAMS FILL IN THE KNOWLEDGE GAP

As a leader, it's important to know what you don't know. How? By engaging with diverse people on your team. If you include a variety of people, then *someone* on your team will be able to help you. That's why I frequently ask members of my team, "What am I missing?" I assume that I'm always missing something, and I believe someone can help me. When they do, then I'm freed up to focus on what I do know and what I do well.

2. DIVERSE TEAMS FILL IN THE PERSPECTIVE GAP

Malcolm Forbes said that diversity is the art of thinking independently together. I love that because getting good independent thinkers to work together is the leadership challenge I love tackling. When everyone thinks and says the same things, it's the end of creativity and death to an entrepreneurial environment.

As a leader, it is my responsibility to encourage and engage in conversations that draw out different perspectives. I don't need or want my team members to parrot back to me what I think or to try to guess what I want. I want to know what *they* think. I want my team to "take me on" when they see things differently. I want them to challenge me just like I challenge them. It is only then that we get the most out of one another. That's called win-win.

3. DIVERSE TEAMS FILL IN THE EXPERIENCE GAP

A little bit of experience outweighs a whole lot of theory as far as I'm concerned. The greater the differences in personal experiences, the greater the team's ability to achieve, and the greater number of "tools" the team has at its disposal. As the saying goes, if all you have is a hammer, everything looks like a nail. Diversity helps prevent us from hammering away at things that need a screwdriver approach.

CONSIDER

What knowledge, perspective, and experience do you lack that would benefit your team or organization? Does your current team have the potential to provide what's needed? If not, what kinds of different people could you recruit to fill these gaps?

_____

_____

_____

_____

BARRIERS TO DIVERSITY

The greatest of leaders seem to embrace diversity instinctively. Winston Churchill, who masterfully led the United Kingdom during the difficult years of World War II, brought political adversaries like Clement Attlee into his strategy meetings in the underground bunker in London. Churchill knew the crisis demanded extraordinary talent, not just the skills of the people he would be comfortable with. Yet, if inviting diversity is such a valuable practice, why don't more leaders embrace it? Because diversity is uncomfortable. Many leaders fail to deal with that discomfort and have a difficult time overcoming these common barriers to diversity:

1. FEAR OF CONFLICT

A diverse team will naturally possess differences of opinion, perspective, and worldview. That almost inevitably leads to conflict. Many people are afraid of that, yet it's a necessary part of life. Conflict can actually help us. Author and consultant Patrick Lencioni wrote about this in his book *The Five Dysfunctions of a Team*:

> All great relationships, the ones that last over time, require productive conflict in order to grow. This is true in marriage, parenthood, friendship, and certainly business.

Unfortunately, conflict is considered taboo in many situations, especially at work. The higher you go up the management chain, the more you find people spending inordinate amounts of time and energy trying to avoid the kind of passionate debates that are essential to any great team.[2]

Lencioni teaches that productive conflict has one purpose: "To produce the best possible solution in the shortest period of time."[3] When different people with different experiences sharing different opinions all sit at the table with the same objective, you can produce extraordinary results. But it requires people to set aside their titles and positions, personal agendas, and preferences. Everyone must want the best ideas to win, not just their own or their group's.

A marriage counselor once shared something with me about resolving the conflicts in marriage. People usually enter a marriage with different personalities, different experiences, different perspectives, and different expectations. Whatever differences existed before the wedding are intensified as the couple lives together for the first time. But happy marriages are based less on compatibility and more on how they deal with incompatibility. Rather than allowing the relationship to get tied up in knots, they need to learn to loosen the knot a bit—to face and resolve conflict.

CONSIDER

Examine these two approaches to conflict. Mark the phrase that best describes you on each line.

UNHEALTHY CONFLICT	HEALTHY CONFLICT
❑ Takes Differences Personally	❑ Sees Differences Impartially
❑ Dumps Personal Baggage	❑ Desires to Know the Person
❑ Searches for Retaliation	❑ Searches for Resolution
❑ Results in Hurt	❑ Results in Helpfulness
❑ Seeks Quick Conclusions	❑ Seeks Understanding
❑ Holds Back from the Conversation	❑ Becomes Part of the Conversation
❑ Values Self Above Solutions	❑ Values Solutions Above Self
❑ Defends Their Territory	❑ Opens Up New Territory
❑ Makes the Team Worse	❑ Makes the Team Better

What people often fear most are breakdowns and that irreparable harm may occur in relationships. But when you value diversity and are genuinely open to the ideas and insights of other people, you open up the possibility of discovering fresh ideas, building a better team, and taking new ground.

2. Insufficient Personal Network

Most people spend time with others like themselves. That often isn't out of prejudice. It's just how people act. When I was growing up, my mother used to tell me, "Birds of a feather flock together." She said it because she wanted me to spend time with other boys of high character, not kids who made bad choices and got into trouble. But the old adage she used to quote also is an indication that people naturally gravitate toward others of similar background, age, and race.

Take an honest look at your peers, friends, and colleagues. If most of the people you know look like you, vote like you, and listen to the same music as you, you probably need to put some work into expanding your network. If you need to expand your personal network, as I did, keep these things in mind:

Expanding Your Network Requires Humility

When I started my leadership career, I thought I was always right. My greatest discovery as I started to meet people unlike myself was that they had so much to offer. Before making the improvement shift, I had shortchanged myself. Realizing that was humbling. When I recognized that others knew what I didn't, and that they had as much to contribute as I did, I could leave my world and enter new ones. Instead of fearing loss, I was anticipating what I would gain from our interaction.

Expanding Your Network Requires Intentionality

If you wait for connections with dissimilar people to happen on their own, they will never happen. You need to get out of your own natural "flock" and migrate to where other birds live and work. It will be uncomfortable, and anything uncomfortable or unusual must be done with high intentionality.

Expanding Your Network Requires Energy

Any time you try something new, it's going to take extra energy. That probably seems like common sense. However, people don't plan for it. If you want to make your team more diverse, gear up for it. Plan to keep going when you're too tired or don't feel like moving forward.

EXPANDING YOUR NETWORK REQUIRES TIME

The same can be said of time. It will take you time to build a diversified team. On top of that, it will take time (and energy) to see the benefits of diversity. You'll need to demonstrate patience as you start the "diversity dance," where you take two steps forward and one step back. It will take time for people to get to know one another. Everyone won't play nice at first. You'll encounter speed bumps and detours. That's true for any good team. But can you get there? Yes, if you give the time and energy required.

EXPANDING YOUR NETWORK REQUIRES LOVE

This one may be a surprise, especially in a business context, but I'm going to tell it like it is. Love makes all things work, and the foundation of love is being willing to value people—including people different from you and people you don't like. I've discovered that the more I value people, the more I add value to them. And the more I add value to them, the more value they return to the team. What gets appreciated, appreciates.

CONSIDER

What is keeping you from expanding your network? Lack of humility? Failure of intentionality? Unwillingness to expend energy or time? Indifference to people? What can you do to change?

_____

_____

_____

_____

_____

_____

_____

3. Unwillingness to Deal with Prejudice

I didn't grow up trying to isolate myself from people who were different from me—I just didn't know many. When I did eventually seek out relationships with people who were different, such as when I began connecting with the African-American business community in Atlanta, I discovered that I possessed a passive prejudice against people who were unlike me. Because of my ignorance, I had a blind spot. I assumed that people like me had good ideas that worked better than anyone else's. Exposure to different people from different backgrounds revealed my prejudice.

There's a saying I came across that really opened my eyes to what happens when you're prejudiced. I don't know who said it, but it's true: "The world is like a hand and all of the people its fingers. If you hate and destroy one group of people, you lose a finger, and the grasp of the world is less."

Embracing diversity has allowed me to have a better grasp of the world around me. My perspective has been changed. Does yours need to be? What prejudices, whether conscious or unknown, do you possess that are keeping you from connecting with people unlike you and diversifying your team? You need to identify whatever is holding you back and work to resolve it.

CONSIDER

The problem with prejudices is they often come from having blind spots, which means you can't see them. However, often there are clues you *can* see. Where do you suspect you may possess prejudices? Explore that. You can't deal with something you don't acknowledge.

_____

_____

_____

_____

_____

_____

_____

_____

4. ARROGANCE

Some leaders are so confident in their own genius that they can't imagine other people adding value to their work. They believe the less similar others are, the less they can contribute. And sadly, the farther down in the organization people are, the more they are ignored. But the reality is that no leaders are so good that they can afford to ignore the contributions of others. No one is indispensable.

If you dismiss the ideas and potential contributions of others, especially those offered by people different from you, you will never reach your potential and neither will your team. And, sadly, you will never even know it!

5. PERSONAL INSECURITIES

There's an old joke that the CEO of an organization met one day with the head of HR and said, "Search the organization for an alert, aggressive young leader who could step into my shoes, and when you find him, fire him." Just as the CEO in that joke felt threatened by strong young leaders, there are people who feel threatened or uncomfortable around those who are different. That personal insecurity is easily sensed by others and puts them off.

The topic of insecurity is a complex one, and if you're an insecure leader, you may need to get help dealing with it. But I will say this: the best antidote I've ever found for personal insecurity is to think about helping other people and putting them first. When you do that, you stop worrying about trying to look good, and you put your attention on making others look good.

THE BEST ANTIDOTE I'VE EVER FOUND FOR PERSONAL INSECURITY IS TO THINK ABOUT HELPING OTHER PEOPLE AND PUTTING THEM FIRST.

If you have insecurities, especially those driven by other's strengths or differences, start working on them. If you don't, your leadership will harm—not help—the team.

CONSIDER

What kinds of people intimidate you? Who brings out the worst in you? Who makes you nervous? Answers to these questions can give you clues about your insecurities. When you think about these people, what are you afraid of?

_____

_____

_____

_____

_____

_____

_____

One of the ways to deal with insecurities is to admit your weaknesses and stop pretending they don't exist. Take some time to face your fears, acknowledge your weaknesses, and appreciate others who are skilled where you are not.

6. FAILING TO BE INCLUSIVE

The final common barrier to promoting team diversity is the leader and team members' failure to be inclusive. When people are on your team but don't feel like they belong or contribute, they disconnect. And they don't bring their best gifts and talents to the table.

For many years I've taught people to seek common ground with others as the way to start the connection process and to further that process by valuing people and adding value to them. I still believe this is the way to start. But the whole idea of _inclusion_ and how it relates to diversity is changing because of millennials. I recently read a study about the approach millennials take to the workplace, and I thought, _No wonder the number one question I'm asked in the business community is how to interact with millennials._

The study was called "The Radical Transformation of Diversity and Inclusion: The Millennial Influence" and was published by Deloitte University. It said that my generation of baby boomers as well as Generation Xers see _inclusion_ as a function of morality—the right thing to do. We would define it in terms of representation, or ensuring fair inclusion of "gender, race, religion, ethnicity, and sexual orientation."[4] In contrast, millennials see diversity and inclusion as having intrinsic value. They allow voices to be heard that have a tangible and beneficial impact on business. The goal isn't just bringing together people of different races, religions, and genders; instead, they want to bring together people with differences in background, personal experience, style, and perspective.[5]

How those people are brought together is also important to millennials. As the study's authors, Christie Smith and Stephanie Turner, explained:

> When it comes to defining inclusion, millennials focus primarily and extensively on teaming, valuing a culture of connectivity, and using collaborative tools to drive business impact. Older generations instead defined inclusion in terms of equality, fairness, and the integration, acceptance, and tolerance of gender, racial, and ethnic diversity within the organization.[6]

Millennials are just happy to have people at the table. They want everyone to be seen as a contributor, and inclusion hasn't occurred until that's been empowered to happen.

Smith and Turner suggested that good leadership supporting inclusion and diversity will help millennials to become fully engaged. Leaders can do that by providing "a collaborative environment in which employees can see the impact of their work, understand the value they bring to the organization, and are recognized for their efforts. Leaders believe in openness and transparency and demonstrate that a cognitively diverse team is better for business."[7]

HOW TO LEADERSHIFT TO DIVERSITY AND INCLUSION

If you're a millennial, you're probably saying, "Amen." If you're a boomer or Gen Xer, you're likely supportive of creating an environment that's diverse and inclusive, but you aren't sure what to do with these different ways of thinking and alternate perspectives. I have three suggestions:

1. CREATE A CULTURE OF SHARING

No matter how diverse the workplace is, teams will not embrace creativity unless there is a culture conducive to interaction and sharing of knowledge. This requires de-emphasizing titles, positions, and roles. It means inviting everyone to speak up. It means giving people opportunities to lead before they have an official role—and sometimes even before you feel they are fully ready. And it means being more open to differences. When you share space, share responsibility, share ownership, and share rewards, everyone wants to contribute.

CONSIDER

How can you make your workplace more open to everyone's input, where you share responsibility, ownership, and rewards?

_____

_____

_____

_____

_____

_____

2. BROADEN YOUR PERSPECTIVE ON DIVERSITY

In an article in *Harvard Business Review*, business psychology professor Tomas Chamorro-Premuzic wrote, "Most discussions about diversity focus on demographic variables (e.g., gender, age, and race). However, the most interesting and influential aspects of diversity are psychological (e.g., personality, values, and abilities)."[8] This is also the way millennials see it.

Equality isn't just about giving everyone the same things; it's also about giving unique people what they need. Bernard Tyson, CEO of Kaiser Permanente, said, "We've evolved from equality to equity. Equality says everybody gets equal. Equity says no, everybody gets what they need. Part of building an inclusive environment is not how you're going to change the person. It's how you're going to change yourself and the environment in which the person is going to be successful."[9] That requires us to think differently and treat diversity differently.

3. PROVIDE SOLID LEADERSHIP FOR DIVERSITY TO BE EFFECTIVE

As much as diversity can help a team, it can also challenge a team. Bringing together a diverse group of people isn't easy. Chamorro-Premuzic pointed out, "The creativity gains produced by higher team diversity are disrupted by the inherent social conflict and decision-making deficits that less homogeneous teams create."[10] Good leadership can help bring strength to both ideation and implementation.

CONSIDER

What qualities and skills do you need in order to invite diverse input and creativity from people while effectively directing people so that the team achieves positive results?

_____

_____

_____

_____

_____

_____

_____

_____

I'm still on the journey when it comes to shifting from uniformity to diversity. Why? Because the way people think is still changing, and I have to keep changing to become a better leader. The greatest shift was from thinking I was right to realizing that people are different but they're not wrong. Once I was able to see from their perspective, I better saw their value, and I became open to it.

There's something of a paradox in all this. To embrace diversity, we must celebrate our differences. But I still believe the way we get there is to look for common ground. In the end, I think we all want the same things: to be heard, to value one another, to work together, to be successful, and to make a difference. If we can connect where we're similar and contribute using our differences, we can accomplish great things.

TEAM UNIFORMITY TO
TEAM DIVERSITY

THE IMPROVEMENT SHIFT

DISCUSSION QUESTIONS

1. What kind of community did you grow up in? Was it diverse or homogeneous? How did your community of origin impact your thinking about people different from you?

2. How much does fear of potential conflict affect your thinking when it comes to embracing diversity and including others who have strongly different perspectives from yours?

3. What challenges have you seen diversity bring to a team? What benefits?

4. How can a leader balance the pursuit of common ground with the promotion of diversity at the same time to obtain positive results on a team?

5. No one wants to think of himself as prejudiced, yet acknowledging prejudice is the first step toward overcoming it. What prejudices do you have toward others that you would like to eliminate? What steps can you take to make this leadershift?

NOTES

LESSON TEN

POSITIONAL AUTHORITY TO
MORAL AUTHORITY

THE INFLUENCE SHIFT

The true measure of leadership is influence—nothing more, nothing less.

THE LAW OF INFLUENCE

I've been known for my definition of leadership for more than forty-five years: leadership is influence. If you've led people for any length of time, you probably know instinctively that this is true. But have you ever wondered where the influence comes from?

No Authority

I found myself asking that question in my first leadership job. Just a few weeks out of college, I became the pastor of a small rural church in the farming community of Hillham, Indiana. The word *community* almost makes it sound bigger than it really was: eleven houses, two gas stations, and a little country store.

It was a job I thought I could handle in an environment where I could learn the ropes. The church wasn't big, it wasn't in a city, and there were no titans of industry to deal with. I would be a medium fish in a small pond. The bylaws of the organization said that I was the leader of the congregation and the chairman of the organization's board. I thought that made me a leader.

The first time I met with the board, I prepared for it. I thought about the vision and how I would articulate it. I thought about how I wanted the meeting to go, and I wrote a detailed agenda.

I knew that, as the chairman, I was supposed to open the meeting and run it. So after the introductions and greetings were finished and we were sitting around the table, I prepared to start. But before I could say or do anything, Claude, one of the board members, said, "Pastor, why don't you open us in prayer?"

That's a good idea, I thought, so I prayed.

I opened up the file folder with copies of my agenda in it and was about to hand them out, when Claude said, "There are a couple of things I think we ought to talk about tonight."

Oh, I thought, *okay. We can take care of those things first. Then we can get to my agenda.*

Claude led the discussion and asked questions while the other men responded. I listened and tried to follow along. Most of the things they were dealing with were the kind of mundane, everyday items that need to be done in an organization, so there was nothing earth-shattering.

After about an hour, Claude said, "Well, that about does it. Pastor, why don't you close us in prayer?"

So I said a prayer, everybody got up, shook hands, said their good-byes, and went home. And I thought to myself, *What just happened?*

WHERE DOES AUTHORITY COME FROM?

That's the day I learned that a leadership position does not give someone leadership authority. And having a title is not the same as having influence. I had the title, but everyone followed Claude. His opinion was the one that mattered at the table. Everyone agreed with everything he said. And they were glad to do what he said.

A LEADERSHIP POSITION DOES NOT GIVE SOMEONE LEADERSHIP AUTHORITY.

Back then, I had not yet discovered my definition of leadership, but after that board meeting, I began thinking about the topic. And I started trying to figure out why all the board members followed Claude. He was a middle-aged farmer who also worked at the nearby power plant. He wasn't an especially impressive man. He wasn't educated. But he had influence.

I look back now, and I realize that in the small world of Hillham, Claude had a degree of moral authority. To the people in that church and on that board, his words carried great weight. Why? Because of the way he lived his life. He was a good man. He was honest, fair, and hardworking. His words and actions lined up, and that had been true for decades. He cared for the congregation and was always ready to help. Claude would not have recognized himself as a leader or called himself a leader, yet he had earned the right to be followed.

When it comes to leadership, I think there are all kinds of authority. Here are some examples:

- *Natural Authority:* Some people naturally lead better than others and therefore step into leadership roles.
- *Positional Authority:* This kind of authority comes with a title or a formal position in an organization and is the lowest level of leadership.
- *Knowledge Authority:* Knowing more than others do or having specific information can give people an influence edge.
- *Situational Authority:* A certain circumstance can arise that requires the most qualified person to lead in that situation.
- *Relational Authority:* When people have built relationships with others, that gives them influence to lead.
- *Proximity Authority:* When individuals are close to the real leader or authority figure, they can borrow from that leader's influence to lead others.

- *Success Authority:* Success gives people credibility, and others want to be on their team to be part of their success.
- *Mentoring Authority:* Developers of other people increase their influence with the people they mentor and gain a reputation for credibility.
- *Seniority Authority:* In some cultures, being an elder or having seniority in an organization gives authority.

My experience with Claude started me on a journey toward understanding different kinds of leadership authority and ultimately led me to the concept of moral authority, which is the highest level of influence. For fifty years I have been in the process of the influence shift, from positional authority to moral authority. It's a journey I'm still on, and a shift I'm still working to make.

What is moral authority? It can be difficult to define. Here's a perspective from Harvard Business School professor Kevin Sharer. He wrote:

> Moral authority is not easy to define precisely, but like many things, you know it when you see it, or especially when you do not. Lack of moral authority in leaders breeds distrust, creates cynicism and kills initiative throughout the organization. Over time, the lack of strong moral authority in the leadership is fatal to the enterprise or country.[1]

These perspectives make moral authority sound grandiose. It can be, but it doesn't have to be. Claude had moral authority and didn't even know it. But so did Nelson Mandela and Mother Teresa. So what is moral authority? Here's my definition:

> Moral authority is the recognition of a person's leadership influence based on who they are more than the position they hold. It is attained by authentic living that has built trust and it is sustained by successful leadership endeavors. It is earned by a lifetime of consistency. Leaders can strive to earn moral authority by the way they live, but only others can grant them moral authority.

Moral authority is truly the highest level of leadership influence, and many people recognize it. It comes from possessing good values. It adds value to others.

It inspires people. It helps the leader to make the right decisions for the right reasons. It marks a life of words and actions that line up. We know when we're in the presence of someone who has moral authority, and we want to follow them!

In an article titled "Four Ways to Build Moral Authority," Chuck Olson said,

> People follow people, not positions. Your business card may say you're a leader and in-charge, but if your bank account of moral authority is overdrawn, you will be forced to rely on extrinsic factors to rally your followers. No amount of skill, wealth, personality, education, or accomplishment can compensate for the absence of moral authority. Perks and paychecks are the currency required to enlist people in a project, but moral authority is the currency required to enlist people in a movement.[2]

Moral authority has the implicit power to transform what is into what can be. It takes people to higher levels of living and leading. It's inspirational, yet at the same time it is grounded and credible. It makes leaders better because they desire to do better. Moral authority brings out the best in teams because of the respect team members have for the leaders and the desire team members have to live up to and follow their example.

The Pathway to Moral Authority

One of the dangers when anyone begins discussing moral authority is that it can sound mystical and out of reach. However, it is grounded in four things: competence, courage, consistency, and character. I believe anyone can pursue moral authority and develop greater influence by developing in all four of these areas. Let's take a look at each of them.

1. Competence—The Ability to Lead Well

Everything starts here. Competence is the core of moral authority. If you can't do your job, if you can't deliver the goods, if you can't lead the team well, why would anyone want to follow you? You can't cultivate moral authority unless people respect you. Author George L. Davis observed, "Authority is not something we buy, are born with, or even have delegated to us by our superiors. It is something we earn—and we earn it from our subordinates. No manager has any real authority over his people until he has proved himself worthy of it—in the eyes of his people—not his own, nor those of his superiors."[3]

COMPETENCE IS THE CORE OF MORAL AUTHORITY.

Doing your work with devotion to excellence and the will to follow through will give you a positive reputation for competence. That's true in any profession. But leaders need to also cultivate influence with others and demonstrate competence in their ability to engage with people and motivate and inspire them to work together. Forty years ago, I started teaching the 5 Levels of Leadership to help people understand how influence worked and to teach them a growth process they could follow to become better leaders. I write about this more fully in my book *Developing the Leader Within You 2.0*, but I want to summarize it here to help you get a feel for how you can develop your leadership competence.

LEVEL 1: POSITION—PEOPLE FOLLOW BECAUSE THEY HAVE TO
The authority someone receives at this level is very limited and is restricted to the leader's job description. A leader need not be competent to receive a leadership appointment. In some organizations, that person doesn't even have to be competent to *retain* a leadership position.

LEVEL 2: PERMISSION—PEOPLE FOLLOW BECAUSE THEY WANT TO
A leader begins to develop authority at this second level. When the leader builds relationships, people are willing to work with them because they like them and enjoy spending time with them. They are beginning to give permission for the person to lead them.

LEVEL 3: PRODUCTION—PEOPLE FOLLOW BECAUSE YOU DEMONSTRATE COMPETENCE
On this level a leader begins to demonstrate genuine competence. Being productive is a big step in gaining moral authority with others. People follow because the leader has produced results and is successful, and they want to be on a winning team.

LEVEL 4: PEOPLE DEVELOPMENT—PEOPLE FOLLOW BECAUSE YOU HELP THEM BECOME COMPETENT

When you start to invest in people and help them to become successful personally, your level of authority rises dramatically, the lives of the people you help improve, and this gives you a level of credibility you can gain no other way.

LEVEL 5: PINNACLE—PEOPLE FOLLOW BECAUSE YOU HAVE A REPUTATION FOR EXCELLENCE

When you live a life of competence, influence people at each of the first four levels, and develop leaders over a long period of time, you can approach the pinnacle of leadership. This is where true moral authority is established.

Moral authority is not based on position, but you must learn the skills of each level of leadership and master them to be seen as highly competent in leadership. However, competence alone is not enough to earn moral authority.

ASSESS

How do you rate your competence in your core work area? On a scale of 1 (poor) to 10 (excellent), how good are you at your job? Circle the number that applies.

1   2   3   4   5   6   7   8   9   10

What one thing could you do immediately to improve your score?

_____

_____

_____

How do you rate your competence when it comes to influencing others on your team or in your organization? On a scale of 1 (positional influence) to 10 (pinnacle influence), how would you score your ability? Circle the number that applies.

1   2   3   4   5   6   7   8   9   10

(continued)

What could you start doing immediately to earn the next level of leadership with members of your team?

_____

_____

_____

_____

_____

2. COURAGE—MOVING FORWARD IN THE FACE OF FEAR

Leadership authority shrinks or expands with a person's courage. Author and professor C. S. Lewis said, "Courage is not simply one of the virtues but the form of every virtue at the testing point." Without courage, you can't live any other virtue consistently. With courage, especially when facing great obstacles, you begin to gain moral authority.

I think everyone admires courage, and intuitively we understand that it carries weight. We can follow a leader who is courageous. More specifically, here's how courage relates to moral authority:

COURAGE ENCOURAGES PEOPLE DURING DIFFICULT AND UNCERTAIN TIMES

There is perhaps no greater need for courage from a leader than during difficult times. Poet Ralph Waldo Emerson is rumored to have said:

> Whatever you do, you need courage. Whatever course you decide upon, there is always someone to tell you [that] you are wrong. There are always difficulties arising, which tempt you to believe that your critics are right. To map out a course of action and follow it to the end, requires some of the same courage which a soldier needs. Peace has its victories, but it takes brave men [and women] to win them.

The courage that people need to see and feel during difficult times does not have to be loud and dramatic, though many times it is. The difficulties of our everyday lives often require us to find and display courage.

COURAGE ENABLES PEOPLE TO MAXIMIZE THEIR POTENTIAL

In *Making the Courage Connection*, Doug Hall wrote, "Courage has a tangible quality. You can't touch it, but you can feel it. It feels like positive acceleration. Courage sends a rush of energy through your body. It makes you wake up in the morning with a feeling of wanting to wrap your hands around the day."[4] Being courageous not only fires you up but also fires up others and makes them more courageous. That's important, because nobody ever reached his or her potential by cowering in fear. Fortune favors the bold.

COURAGE HELPS LEADERS FIND THEIR VOICE

As leaders display courage in crisis, they often find their voices. During World War II, when England stood alone against Nazi Germany, Winston Churchill found his voice. In 1940 while addressing Parliament, he told his countrymen, "We shall never surrender." Martin Luther King Jr. found his voice during the civil rights struggle of the 1960s. His words still resound today: "Our lives begin to end the day we remain silent about things that matter."

Every leader who possesses moral authority has had to stand alone at some point in time. Such moments make leaders. Such stands are often very difficult, but when leaders look back afterward, they often see those as their proudest moments.

We don't choose the times or the circumstances we must face in life, but we do choose our responses. I love the prayer of the Special Olympics because I think it represents the mind-set we should embrace as leaders: "Let me win, but if I cannot win, let me be brave in the attempt."

ASSESS

How do you rate your courageousness? On a scale of 1 (meek) to 10 (bold), how willing are you to step up and do what's right when you're afraid? Circle the number that applies.

| 1 | 2 | 3 | 4 | 5 | 6 | 7 | 8 | 9 | 10 |

(continued)

In what area of your life are you currently displaying too little courage? What one thing could you do immediately to improve your level of courage in that area?

_____

_____

_____

3. CONSISTENCY—DOING WELL ALL THE TIME, NOT JUST SOMETIMES

In his fantastic book *Visioneering*, Andy Stanley described the value of consistency related to moral authority. He wrote:

> It is the alignment between a person's convictions and his behavior that makes his life persuasive. Herein is the key to sustained influence. . . .
>
> Moral authority is the credibility you earn by walking your talk . . . It is the relationship other people see between what you say and what you do, between what you claim to be and what you are. A person with moral authority is beyond reproach. That is, when you look for a discrepancy between what he says he believes and what he does, you come up empty. There is alignment between conviction and action, belief and behavior.
>
> Nothing compensates for a lack of moral authority. No amount of communication skills, wealth, accomplishment, education, talent, or position can make up for a lack of moral authority. We all know plenty of people who have those qualities but who exercise no influence over us whatsoever. Why? Because there is a contradiction between what they claim to be and what we perceive them to be.[5]

What Stanley described is internal consistency between values and actions, which is essential to a leader's success if he or she desires to gain moral authority. Equally important is the ability to be consistent over time.

Consistency compounds over time. If you do the right things when you're young, it mostly goes unnoticed and unrecognized. But if you do the right things and lead well over decades, it becomes recognized, and you get more credit than you feel you deserve. That's the power of what I call layered living. If you embrace layered learning (as I described in Lesson 3 on shifting from goals to growth) and you practice layered leadership (by consistently living out your values and performing with excellence), then your reward can be layered living, where you reap the benefits of moral authority.

Consistency is so valuable to a leader that it's difficult to list all its benefits. Here are just a few:

- *Consistency establishes your reputation.* Nearly anyone can be good once. Being good continually is difficult. However, continued repetition leads to a positive reputation.
- *Consistency makes team members more secure.* Perhaps the greatest compliment a person can receive is, "I can depend on you." A consistent leader inspires team members to become more confident.
- *Consistency allows for accurate measurement of your growth.* It's difficult to gauge the progress of inconsistent people. The track record we establish shows what we have done and how far we have come.
- *Consistency makes you relevant.* People who bounce back and forth between engagement and disengagement always have to play catch-up. By staying consistently engaged, you don't fall behind.
- *Consistency models your expectations for others.* When you consistently model your values and work ethic, team members know what you expect of them because they've seen it every day. Consistency always reinforces expectations.
- *Consistency maintains your message.* When a leader communicates a vision but acts in ways that are inconsistent with that vision the result is confusion. It distracts from the message and makes it more difficult for everyone on the team.

ASSESS

How do you rate when it comes to consistency? On a scale of 1 (poor) to 10 (excellent), how would you score yourself? Circle the number that applies.

| 1 | 2 | 3 | 4 | 5 | 6 | 7 | 8 | 9 | 10 |

(continued)

What prevents you from scoring higher in this area? What one thing could you
do immediately to improve your consistency?

_____

_____

_____

_____

_____

Consistency, along with competence and courage, is vital to a leader's ability
to develop moral authority, but there's still one more component without which
moral authority is impossible to earn.

4. CHARACTER—BEING BIGGER ON THE INSIDE THAN THE OUTSIDE

Moral authority is a result of right intentions, right values, right beliefs, right
actions, right relationships, and right responses. There is a lot to do right to develop moral authority. That doesn't mean perfection. We are all human and make
mistakes. But to have moral authority, our intentions must be right; the motives
of the heart must be good.

While much of leadership is outward and public, the right motives and the
good character traits we need to become leaders with moral authority are won
in private. These two aspects of leadership, public and private, resemble the two
parts of a tree. One part you see: our public leadership is like a tree's trunk and
branches. That's the part that bears fruit. However, who leaders are in private is
what can't be seen, like a tree's roots. If the roots are shallow, then the tree won't
survive. Drought will dry it up. A storm will knock it down. But if the roots are
deep, the tree can thrive in almost any circumstance.

What does it mean to develop deep roots as a leader? It means having strong
character. What kind of character does a leader need to have? I believe good character demonstrates these four characteristics:

INTEGRITY

I define integrity two ways. First, it's the alignment of your values and actions. You know what's right and you do it. Leaders with moral authority hold

themselves to a high standard of conduct. The second definition has to do with decision-making. Leaders of integrity do the right thing, even when it's hard, even when it's not best for them personally. They put the team, the organization, and the vision ahead of themselves.

LEADERS OF INTEGRITY DO THE RIGHT THING, EVEN WHEN IT'S HARD, EVEN WHEN IT'S NOT BEST FOR THEM PERSONALLY.

AUTHENTICITY

Author and spiritual leader Mark Batterson said, "Authenticity is the new authority in leadership." I agree, because I believe that is an essential part of moral authority. People do not want to follow leaders who pretend to be what they're not. They don't expect perfection—just honesty.

This can be a real struggle for many leaders. They want to meet others' expectations and can be tempted to compromise their beliefs or standards. But to be the best leader you can be, you need to acknowledge who you really are and be willing to let people witness your authenticity.

HUMILITY

I believe humility is an essential quality for a leader who possesses moral authority. My friend Rick Warren said, "Humility is not denying your strengths. Humility is being honest about your weaknesses." No matter how you define *humility*, know that it means three things. First, you possess self-awareness and can criticize yourself. Second, you are confident and comfortable enough that you don't feel any need to draw attention to yourself. And third, you revel in the accomplishments of others and are eager to help them shine.

LOVE

The final character quality to embrace as a leader in order to have moral authority is love. You must care about people. You must respect them. You must value them. People can always tell when you don't, and that creates an instant disconnection that short-circuits moral authority.

What do you want to do with your leadership? I think every leader wants to make an impact, a difference. It's the reason we get up in the morning. It's why we work with people. It's why we create teams or build organizations. Do you have it in you to do something big? Do you want to change your organization, or your community, or your culture, or your country? How big are your dreams? The bigger they are, the more you need moral authority to accomplish them.

When I was in my early thirties, I started to get the sense that my leadership could be impactful and my life could make a difference. That prompted me to make some personal decisions. At the time, I simply thought they were the right things to do to be a better leader. Today, I can see that they helped me in the four areas I've written about in this lesson: competence, courage, consistency, and character. I decided to:

1. Always put people first.
2. Live to make a difference, not to make money.
3. Be myself, but be my best self possible.
4. Express gratitude—reject entitlement.
5. Be willing to be misunderstood and lonely for the right reasons.

I've worked hard to follow these guidelines for the last forty years.

In the end, you don't get to grant yourself moral authority. You can choose to strive for it, but only others can give it to you, and they must do so freely. But that should not stop you from doing everything right that you can to earn it. Because if you gain moral authority, it makes you worthy of respect, inspires trust and confidence, and enables you to lead at the highest standards of performance. This leadershift will increase your influence, giving you buy-in not only from the people on your team but from others who aren't under your formal leadership. And with that influence, there's no telling what you can help people accomplish.

POSITIONAL AUTHORITY TO
MORAL AUTHORITY

THE INFLUENCE SHIFT

DISCUSSION QUESTIONS

1. What value do you think moral authority has for a leader? What benefits do you think it would give you? What would you attempt to accomplish with it?

2. What kinds of authority do you most often rely upon to get things done? Why do you use them?

   - Natural Authority
   - Knowledge Authority
   - Relational Authority
   - Success Authority
   - Seniority Authority

   - Positional Authority
   - Situational Authority
   - Proximity Authority
   - Mentoring Authority

3. Which component of mortal authority have you found to be the easiest to achieve: competence, courage, consistency, or character? Which have you found to be the most difficult?

4. How would you prioritize the importance of the four components: competence, courage, consistency, or character? Explain your answer.

5. What one specific step are you willing to take in order to improve in the area that you believe to be the most important of the four? How and when will you do it?

NOTES

TRAINED LEADERS TO
TRANSFORMATIONAL LEADERS

THE IMPACT SHIFT

If your actions inspire people to dream more, learn more, do more, and become more, then you are a transformational leader.

Of all the lessons in this book, this one is the most important. Why do I say that? Because if you make only one leadershift in your life, this is the one I would wish for you to choose. The impact shift from trained leaders to transformational leaders will bring the greatest change to your life and the lives of those around you.

If your actions inspire people to dream more, learn more, do more, and become more, then you are a transformational leader. You influence people to think, speak, and act in ways that make a positive difference in their lives and the lives of others. That kind of leadership can change the world!

MY CHANGE IN LEADERSHIP PERSPECTIVE

My leadershift from trained leader to transformational leader occurred early. This story is very personal to me, and it had a dramatic effect on my life. At the heart of this shift was my faith, which is at the foundation of who I am. However,

I value you whether or not you are a person of faith. No matter what your perspective is about faith, I don't want you to miss this, so I'll condense my story down to its essence.

At the beginning of my career, I cared mostly about myself and building my organization. Sadly, people were not my top priority. I regret to say that my selfishness sometimes kept me from doing the right thing. There was one particular incident that made me realize that my priorities were wrong. I failed to help a man because I was focused on myself. Then the man died. My selfish decision meant that he never got the help I should have given him, and there was nothing I could do to fix that.

I can't express the devastating impact this had on me. I felt terrible, and it caused me to spend several months reevaluating myself as a leader. For the first time in my life, I started to ask myself the hard questions about my motives and methods that every leader ought to ask. And I was not satisfied with my answers.

During the next few months, I spent a lot of time in prayer and reflection, and I resolved to become a different kind of leader—someone different from whom I had been up to that time. Thankfully my heart was changed, and my actions started following my heart. I became a person who valued other people and demonstrated that through my leadership decisions, which made others my top priority. The change within me was deep and made a difference that still influences me today. If I hadn't made this shift, my leadership would have been hollow and self-centered. I credit this with making possible whatever difference I've made with my leadership.

ESSENTIALS FOR TRANSFORMATIONAL LEADERSHIP

I'm a firm believer in training in leadership. I've done it myself for fifty years and helped others for more than forty years. But I also recognize there's a huge difference between trained leaders and leaders who are transformational.

For many years I have studied transformational movements and the people who led them. I've identified five actions common to all of them. If you desire to make the impact shift from trained leader to transformational leader, start doing these too.

CONSIDER

Take a look at the following comparison between trained leaders and transformational leaders. Mark the phrase on each line that best describes you.

TRAINED LEADERS	TRANSFORMATIONAL LEADERS
❑ Know How to Lead	❑ Know Why They Lead
❑ Are Liked	❑ Are Contagious
❑ Influence Today	❑ Influence Today and Tomorrow
❑ Ask People to Follow	❑ Ask People to Make a Difference
❑ Love to Lead	❑ Love the People They Lead
❑ Are Trained	❑ Are Trained and Transformed
❑ Help People	❑ Help People Change
❑ Have a Career	❑ Have a Calling
❑ Impact a Few	❑ Impact Many

1. Possess a Clear Picture of What Transformational Leaders Do

On the surface, all transformational leaders look different from one another. They come in all sizes and shapes, from many races and nationalities, and with a variety of skills and talents. Their differences are many. However, there are a few characteristics that all of them share, and if you desire to become transformational, you must embrace them, too, so that you know what you're striving for:

Transformational Leaders See Things Others Do Not See

Many people see problems and shake their heads. They experience adversity and throw up their hands. They look at challenges and ask "Why?"—not seeking a solution, just venting frustration. When they encounter problems, they see no possibilities. They become victims of negative circumstances and cannot help themselves or others.

Transformational leaders see things differently. They ask, "Why not?" because they're always thinking about trying to create a better future. They see more than others see. Of course, they see the problems. They may even be surrounded by them. But they also see potential in those problems. They believe there is always an answer, a solution, a better way, a brighter future. That belief creates anticipation, not desperation, during the darkest of hours.

How we view things determines how we do things. My friend Dave Ramsey said, "Organizations are not limited by their opportunity; they are limited by their leader." If we don't see the things others don't, how can we lead them to a better future?

ORGANIZATIONS ARE NOT LIMITED BY THEIR OPPORTUNITY; THEY ARE LIMITED BY THEIR LEADER.

DAVE RAMSEY

TRANSFORMATIONAL LEADERS SAY THINGS OTHERS DO NOT SAY
Transformational leaders speak up. They leverage their influence by speaking bold words about a better future. Their voice becomes a tool of transformation. Think of the bold words said by transformational leaders who were willing to describe a better future. Martin Luther King Jr. said, "I have a dream." It took courage for him to be the voice of change when others opposed him.

As I have become a better communicator, I've tried to use my voice to facilitate positive change. At times I was misunderstood. But I made decisions that I believed were right, such as when . . .

- I stood on the floor of a national meeting and promoted a policy of inclusiveness that I knew had no chance of passing.
- I said no to becoming the new host of a prestigious national radio show because I declined to sign a doctrinal statement I didn't agree with.
- I handed back a million-dollar gift given to my nonprofit organization because I proposed going in a direction that the donor did not like.
- I changed the nonprofit EQUIP from a training organization to a transformational one.

None of these decisions was popular when I shared it, and not everyone understood. But sometimes that's what a leader must do. Say things others won't.

Transformational Leaders Believe Things Others Do Not Believe

Transformational leaders believe that they can make a difference. That becomes their passion. President John F. Kennedy said he believed that everyone had a change-the-world speech in them. I was thirteen years old when he said it, and I can still remember how I felt when I heard those words. Although I was only a young teenager, I felt that he was talking directly to me. I believed him—because he believed it.

> ## Everyone has a change-the-world speech in them.
> ### John F. Kennedy

Believing you can make a difference changes everything. When transformational leaders believe that their cause can make a difference, then they bring conviction to their leadership. Without this conviction, you may be able to get people to follow you, and you can be a good leader. But only when you understand that the higher calling of leadership is to get people to follow your cause can you become a great leader.

Transformational leaders believe in others. They are belief magnets. People are drawn to them because they believe in their message and believe it will help people. They rally people together to make a difference; they extend their hand and ask others to join them in their mission. Transformational leaders are belief-makers who help people to believe in themselves.

Transformational Leaders Feel Things Others Do Not Feel

Peter Marshall said, "A different world cannot be built by indifferent people." Passion creates energy and tenacity in people. It fires up leaders and the people who join them for their cause. That fire helps them endure, the way Gandhi did in his fight for Indian independence. It was a process that took fifty-four years. During that time Gandhi fought through attacks, rejection, imprisonment, misrepresentation, and sickness with malaria. And then he was finally victorious. Passion carried him forward.

A DIFFERENT WORLD CANNOT BE BUILT BY INDIFFERENT PEOPLE.

PETER MARSHALL

I've seen passion emerge in the lives of people I lead, and it has changed their lives and the way they lead. This happens every time I invite a group of John Maxwell Team coaches to go with me to another country to train roundtable facilitators. Hundreds of coaches have volunteered to travel overseas, paid all their own expenses, trained twelve hours a day, then traveled in less-than-ideal circumstances to help others. They give up their time, their money, and their energy to do it. And they love it! They tirelessly give of themselves, and yet at the end I hear over and over that they feel they've received more than they gave. And they want to do it again. Paul Martinelli, president of the John Maxwell Team, said, "When the light goes on in your life, you want to turn everyone else's light on." I love that, and it's true. Transformational leaders have their lights on, and they want to help others turn theirs on.

TRANSFORMATIONAL LEADERS DO THINGS OTHERS DO NOT DO
While fear causes many people to shrink back from the unknown and avoid challenges that lie ahead, it causes transformational leaders to prepare and work harder. How do they overcome their fears? By tapping into their sense of purpose and by believing in a cause that is much bigger than themselves. They want to make a difference, and the only questions they need to answer are, "What kind of difference can I make?" and "How big of a difference can it be?" Their strong sense of purpose propels them to do what others aren't willing to do.

I've already mentioned that my greatest desire is to see a country transformed so much that the leaders and citizens acknowledge the positive change. That is a BHAG (Big Hairy Audacious Goal). And I may not live to see it happen. So why am I doing everything I can to be part of this? Because I would rather try something big that is almost impossible than something small that won't make a difference. If you want to make the leadershift from trained to transformational leadership, I encourage you to have a similarly audacious attitude.

CONSIDER

Do you have a clear vision of a way to help others and make a difference? If so, describe it. If not, dream a little. Look where your passion, your current opportunities, and people's needs come together.

_____

_____

_____

_____

_____

_____

2. FOCUS ON YOUR OWN TRANSFORMATION BEFORE LEADING OTHERS TO IT

In Lesson 3 I discussed how I developed the acronym R-E-A-L, with the *E* representing *equipping*. As soon as I understood how important equipping was, I studied the process and discovered the best way to train others. I came up with a five-step process that works no matter what task you're trying to equip another person to do.

1. I do it.
2. I do it, and you are with me.
3. You do it, and I am with you.
4. You do it.
5. You do it, and someone is with you.

Why do I mention this? Because I want you to notice that the process begins with *I do it*. If I want to help others be transformational, I must first be transformed. I cannot give what I do not have. Neither can you.

The first person you must lead will always be you. If you want to see positive changes in your world, the first person you must change is you. As leaders, you and I have to be changed to bring change. We teach what we know, but we reproduce who we are.

Before I personally experienced the transformation of shifting from a desire to make my life successful to a desire to help other people's lives improve, it never entered my mind that I could be a catalyst for positive change. It never entered my heart either. There was no passion within me to help others experience positive change. However, when I began to experience positive change in my life and became less selfish, I was eager to share what was happening with others. Knowing that I was changing got me excited about helping others change too.

If you want to lead any positive change, you need to realize this: transformation begins with you. If you are not willing to change, you are not going to be able to help anyone else.

Philosopher and author James Allen wrote, "Men are anxious to improve their circumstances, but are unwilling to improve themselves; they therefore remain bound." If you want to lead positive change, don't remain bound. Be willing to change within. Start with you. That's always the first step to making a difference.

CONSIDER

What needs to change in you before you will be able to help others make significant changes? Where do you need to be transformed? What steps can you take immediately to begin that transformation process?

_____

_____

_____

_____

_____

_____

3. TAKE POSITIVE ACTION BASED ON YOUR INTERNAL CHANGES

An essential step in the leadershift from trained to transformational is a commitment to taking action. For real change to occur, we must go from knowing to doing. It's at this point that transformation becomes difficult, yet the results are so beautiful. It's difficult because saying is always easier than doing. It's beautiful because action is what brings transformation.

Everything worthwhile in life is uphill—all the way. Transformation requires us to walk uphill. Everyday. All the way. Most people are unwilling to commit to that. Instead of climbing, they would rather be . . .

- *Talking:* "Let's discuss uphill climbing."
- *Thinking:* "Let's contemplate uphill climbing."
- *Planning:* "Let's strategize about uphill climbing."
- *Surveying:* "Let's ask others what they think about uphill climbing."
- *Studying:* "Let's examine what uphill climbing looks like."
- *Resting:* "Let's conserve energy before we start climbing."

Transformation is a result of application, not education. That's why Gandhi said, "An ounce of practice is worth more than tons of preaching." To lead transformationally, you must first live transformed. That takes courage, the courage to let go of the familiar and set off on a better way.

ASSESS

How inclined are you to take action? On a scale of 1 (thinker) to 10 (doer), how would you score yourself? Circle the number that applies.

1   2   3   4   5   6   7   8   9   10

If you scored below 7, what holds you back? How can you become more proactive? If you scored 8 or higher, what one thing could you do to improve by one point?

_____

_____

_____

_____

_____

_____

4. CREATE AN ENVIRONMENT THAT PROMOTES POSITIVE CHANGE

For years I have encouraged people to embrace positive change. More recently my nonprofit organizations have dedicated themselves to promoting transformation. Our experience working with tens of thousands of people has helped us to understand what creates an ideal environment. These are the essentials:

LEADERS WHO ARE PASSIONATE ABOUT TRANSFORMATION

Jim Collins said, "Transformational movements require transformational leaders." Only transformational leaders can bring about transformation. What I've said for years is true: everything rises and falls on leadership.

This poem by Lawrence Tribble really says it all:

One man awake, awakens another.
The second awakens his next-door brother.
The three awake can rouse a town
By turning the whole place upside down.
The many awake can cause such a fuss
It finally awakens the rest of us.
One man up with dawn in his eyes
Surely then multiplies.[1]

Some man or woman has to start that process. The person who does is a transformational leader.

RESOURCES THAT TEACH GOOD VALUES

Many people are unaware that there is a better way to live. They are stuck in the life they have because they are not sure where to go, nor do they know how to move beyond their current situation. I'm convinced from personal experience and observation that good values are the road to a better life. And placing resources that teach good values in the hands of people turns the light on for them so that they can see a better way.

Good values are teachable and reachable. Just one good value in a person's life can bring great benefit. Here are some of the values my nonprofit organizations have helped people to understand and embrace over the years:

- *Attitude:* your attitude colors everything in your life
- *Commitment:* it separates doers from dreamers
- *Competence:* the shortest path to credibility is competence
- *Forgiveness:* forgiveness empowers you to live with a light heart
- *Initiative:* you cannot experience success unless you start
- *Integrity:* living with integrity leads to a life of wholeness
- *Personal Growth:* people who keep learning always have a future
- *Priorities:* clear priorities show you what to do and where to go
- *Relationships:* the quality of your relationships determines the quality of your life
- *Work Ethic:* working hard brings inner satisfaction every day

We've created resources to help people explore ideas, examine themselves, and decide how they will take action to embrace good values and change their lives. If you desire to shift from trained leader to transformational leader, you need to give people resources to help them. Most people cannot find the pathway to a better life without help.

SMALL GROUPS WHERE PEOPLE LEARN AND PARTICIPATE

Too often, training that begins in our heads stays in our heads. We learn something new, but we don't apply it to our lives or put it into practice. That's why transformation needs a living laboratory to be effective. That occurs best in a small group of people where all the members of the group share ideas, speak about themselves with candor and honesty, state their intentions, and hold one another accountable.

EQUIP and the John Maxwell Leadership Foundation, the two nonprofit organizations I founded, use roundtables in small groups to facilitate change. We've found that groups of four to ten can create the perfect environment for people to develop relationships, get to know themselves and others, and experience growth. Most people do not have a high level of self-awareness. They spend so much time and energy projecting a positive image that they don't examine themselves and their motives as much as they could. A safe small-group environment where people see the others as peers, everyone is asked to participate, and the leader of the group is open and authentic about his or her shortcomings encourages everyone to participate, ask questions, listen, share, reflect, and commit to taking action. And if members of the group report back the next time they meet to honestly share both failures and success, everyone is encouraged to grow and change.

I've experienced the positive power of participating in small groups in my own life. Some of the greatest changes that have determined my most important decisions occurred in small-group setting. I wasn't *expecting* these things to happen, but once I committed to a group and fully engaged in the process, good things began to occur. Small groups can bring big growth.

COMMITMENT TO REPRODUCE LEADERS

By definition, for someone to be a leader, he or she must have followers. If you think you're leading but no one is following you, then you're only taking a walk. However, it's not enough to gather followers. To be transformational, leaders must develop and reproduce leaders.

I started to learn this lesson more than thirty years ago when I was leading Skyline Church. We recognized the transformative power of small groups, so we started a small-group program. Naïvely, we thought we could simply put people together in groups and they would flourish. We quickly discovered that if we didn't train leaders, the groups didn't succeed. So we dismantled the program, started training leaders, and relaunched. We were successful this second go-round, but then we learned something else: trained leaders could sustain a group, but transformed leaders could gather, grow, and reproduce groups. They could train other leaders who reached other people and trained other leaders.

When this happens repeatedly, individual transformation leads to group transformation which leads to community transformation. It starts with transformed leaders who want to lead others to transformation.

5. COMMIT TO MAKING A DIFFERENCE WITH OTHERS IN YOUR COMMUNITY

Making positive changes requires commitment from leaders who want to make a difference. Civil rights leader Walter E. Fauntroy eloquently expressed this in an inspiring speech he delivered at Howard University. He said:

> The past is yours. Learn from it. The future is yours. Fulfill it. Knowledge is yours. Use it. Cancer is yours. Cure it. Racism is yours. End it. Injustice is yours. Correct it. Sickness is yours. Heal it. Ignorance is yours. Banish

it. War is yours. Stop it. Hope is yours. Confirm it. America is yours. Save it. The world is yours. Serve it. The dream is yours. Claim it.

Don't be blinded by prejudice, disheartened by the times, or discouraged by the system. Face the system. Challenge it. Change it. Confront it. Correct it. Don't let anything paralyze your mind, tie your hands, or defeat your spirit. Take the world—not to dominate it, but to deliver it. Not to exploit it, but to enrich it—take your dream and inherit the earth.[2]

Change does not happen unless transformational leaders commit themselves to making a difference in their community and invite others to join them in the process. All transformational movements follow a pattern. They occur:

- *Top-Down*—Leadership influence filters down, not up.
- *Small to Big*—Mass movements begin with a few people.
- *Inside Out*—Inner values determine outward behavior.

If you're willing to commit to changing yourself, inviting a small group of people to join you in the process, and preparing other leaders to become agents of transformation, you can change your world.

TAKE ACTION

If you're ready to make a difference and start changing the world, then take action.

Change Yourself: What transformation needs to occur within you (or has already occurred within you) to qualify you to help others experience transformation?

_____

_____

_____

_____

_____

Invest in a Small Group of People: Who can you help? Who do you know who is open to growth and change that would benefit from being in a group you lead? What material or resources could you use that would help them to grow? When will you invite them? When will you start the group?

_____

_____

_____

_____

_____

Develop Other Leaders: Of the people you plan to invite into your group, who has leadership skills or leadership potential? Make additional investment into those people and prepare them to become transformational leaders.

_____

_____

_____

_____

_____

AMAZING TRANSFORMATION

I want to close this lesson with a story told to me by my good friend Jerry Anderson. Jerry was a serial entrepreneur who kept failing until he met John Schrock, a successful businessman who lived his life in accordance with positive values he'd learned by reading Proverbs. Jerry was mentored by John, and it transformed his life. Jerry went on to become highly successful himself, and out of gratitude and a desire to make a difference, he started teaching the values he had learned from John to others. When his efforts started to gain momentum, Jerry founded the nonprofit organization La Red to multiply his efforts.

In the early 2000s, Jerry's organization was invited to Colombia. The reason? The prisons of Colombia were notoriously corrupt at that time. They were run by organized crime and the most powerful inmates. The prisoners were organized and often armed. Money flowed into the prisons. Some of the more powerful inmates had set up suites. A few were even equipped with doors to the outside so that associates and women could come and go at will, bringing money and drugs, among other things.

This criminal environment bred corruption among the guards. Since they could not beat the inmates, they simply joined them. They served the wealthiest criminals and treated the other inmates like slaves. The prison system was brutal. On average, there was a murder every day within the 143 prisons. Jerry said in one instance, a man's head had been cut off and used as a soccer ball in the prison yard.

The Colombian government desired change, but they weren't sure what to do or how to start. They knew they would not be able to change the prison with more guns or new buildings. What they needed to do was change the hearts and minds of the leaders. To do that, they invited Jerry's organization La Red into the prison system to work with the guards.

La Red introduced character development and values into 143 prisons, believing they could transform the culture of the prison by teaching the guards and other prison employees character-based values. They met regularly in small roundtable groups. Any employee who refused to participate in the weekly meeting lost his job.

Slowly, the culture of the prison began to transform. The eleven thousand guards in the prisons were changing. They no longer embraced corruption. They started treating people better. They asked others to forgive their previous behavior. They started to regain their dignity. The change was so dramatic that prisoners started writing letters to the director asking for the same training that the guards were receiving.

What happened next was remarkable. The guards started to allow one prisoner to become part of a roundtable group of guards. To participate, that inmate had to agree to lead his own group with other prisoners in his cell block. The process began with fifty-six prisoners. As these individuals were trained in values, their thinking changed. Their values changed. Their actions changed. They were transformed by the time they started their own groups in their cell blocks. As they led their groups, many of the inmates who were receiving training in the small roundtable groups started to change too. Over several years the entire prison system and its eighty thousand inmates were transformed. Many of the inmates expressed that if they had learned these values earlier in life, they probably would not have ended up in prison. Perhaps most remarkable of all, the murder rate in the prison went from an average of one per day down to one per year!

The success Jerry had in the prisons was so dramatic that the Colombian military invited La Red to train their military troops in character development. The governments of other countries contacted him too. The last time I asked Jerry, he said La Red has helped people in forty-four nations. He estimates that more than one million people have participated in the transformational small groups they offer. And they're still going strong. That's the power of the impact shift. If you leadershift from trained to transformational leadership, there's no telling what kind of impact you can make or how far your influence will go.

TRAINED LEADERS TO
TRANSFORMATIONAL LEADERS

THE IMPACT SHIFT

DISCUSSION QUESTIONS

1. Do you agree that transformation needs to occur in a leader before he or she can lead others to experience transformation? Explain. What difference does it make?

2. Which do you think usually occurs first: discovering of the need for transformation within the community or transformation within the leader prompting him or her to reach out to the community?

3. Do you believe you have the potential to lead positive change within a large or small community? Why?

4. What problem or injustice bothers you the most? Where do you see the greatest need for transformation in your community?

5. What are you willing to attempt to make a difference for people you care about?

NOTES

LESSON TWELVE

CAREER TO
CALLING

THE PASSION SHIFT

Some wake up to an alarm. Some wake up to a calling.

UNKNOWN

This last leadershift should be the most natural shift a person can make, yet many people miss it. They are so busy with their day-to-day existence and with making a living that they don't think about it. Or they've been told that life has no greater meaning—and they actually believed it. I'm here to tell you that this leadershift is available to you if you're willing to reach for it.

WHAT DO YOU DO?

I want to start by asking you a question: How do you currently think about what you do for a living? Yale professor Amy Wrzesniewski has done research with employees in the workplace and observed that people tend to fall into three groups.

What's remarkable is that individuals fall into these three categories regardless of the industry they work in, the social status of their profession, their pay, or their title. For example, in a study, roughly equal numbers of administrative assistants surveyed fell into these three categories. And employees who mopped floors in a hospital were equally likely to fall evenly into these three groups.[1] Think about which best describes you.

1. YOU DO A JOB

When you have a job, your main goal is often to earn a living and support your family. You may not think about it beyond the time you spend on the clock. You may do your job with excellence or you may simply mark time, but either way, when you finish your day or your shift, you walk away and don't think about it. Satisfaction and fulfillment for people who have a job-only mind-set comes from activities outside of work. And while people in this group may hope to advance, they don't think in terms of a strategy of career building.

It's been said that if you choose a job you love, you will never have to work a day in your life. I think that's good advice, but it should be a starting point, not an ending goal. A job is not your calling, no matter how much money it will allow you to make or how it allows you to serve people. A job is merely a vehicle with the potential to take you toward your calling. That's the way you should think of it.

2. YOU BUILD A CAREER

Most people would acknowledge that it's a step forward to think in terms of developing a career rather than just holding a job. When you have a career, the implication is that you are headed in a direction. You're making progress attaining positive achievements. An upward trajectory of skill mastery, larger responsibilities, and greater earnings are all marks of a successful career.

3. YOU FULFILL YOUR CALLING

Author Frederick Buechner said that our purpose is at "that place where your deep gladness meets the world's deep need." Your calling, when you find and embrace it, will result in the merging of your skills, your talents, your character traits, and yourexperiences. It will make use of your experience, your gifts, and the lessons you've learned. It will be represented by a deep desire to create, lead, inspire, and make a difference.

CONSIDER

Take a look at the difference between a career and a calling. Mark the box on each line that best describes you.

CAREER
- ❑ Mainly About You
- ❑ Something You Choose
- ❑ Separated from Your Best Life
- ❑ You Can Take or Leave It
- ❑ Something You Can Do
- ❑ Measured by Success

CALLING
- ❑ Mainly About Others
- ❑ Something Chosen for You
- ❑ Integrated into Your Entire Life
- ❑ Never Leaves You
- ❑ Something You Must Do
- ❑ Measured by Significance

Wouldn't you like to find and fulfill a calling that makes a difference and gets you excited every day for the rest of your life? Finding your calling is like finding your *why*—the reason you exist, your purpose for living. When you do, it changes everything:

- When you find your Why—you find your Way.
- When you find your Why—you find your Will.
- When you find your Why—you find your Wings.

Your life will never be the same once you know what you're called to do and are working to fulfill it every day.

WE ARE ALL SEARCHERS

I believe *everyone* has the potential to find and fulfill his or her purpose. Everyone has the ability to be called. In each of us there is a desire to know more and be more. There is something in us that calls to something bigger. Richard Leider, author, coach, and founder of Inventure, the Purpose Company, has written extensively on the subjects of purpose and calling. He said:

The search for callings is not a trend. It is something much deeper. If it needs a label, it is searcher. James Kavanaugh captured the essence of the drive when he wrote, "I am one of the searchers. There are, I believe, millions of us. We are not unhappy, but neither are we really content. We continue to explore life, hoping to uncover its ultimate secret."

We humans are searchers for meaning. . . . Work has meaning if it serves others. Calling joins self and service. As Aristotle said, "Where our talents and the needs of the world cross, there lies our vocation."[2]

WHERE OUR TALENTS AND THE NEEDS OF THE WORLD CROSS, THERE LIES OUR VOCATION.

ARISTOTLE

THE DAY I WAS CALLED

It's never too early, nor is it ever too late to find your purpose, your calling. I consider myself to be fortunate because I received my calling when I was twenty-nine years old. I was old enough to appreciate it and young enough to have plenty of time to make the most of it. I want to tell you about the experience. Because I'm a person of faith, my experience involves God. However, you do not need to be a person of faith to receive a calling. You just need to be open and watchful.

I experienced my unique calling on July 4, 1976. I was speaking in celebration of the United States' bicentennial, and suddenly I had a clear and compelling sense that God wanted me to invest my life in developing leaders and teaching leadership. It was perhaps the greatest moment of clarity I've ever had in my life.

On the drive home, I told Margaret about it. She listened, as she always does when I'm excited by an idea. She asked, "What are you going to do?"

"Nothing," I answered.

She was surprised, because back then I usually dove right into strategy mode and started creating my plans. But this was different from any other experience

I'd had. Yes, I was excited. I couldn't wait to train leaders for the rest of my life. At the same time, I was also patient, and I felt very settled—calm.

"If this is a calling," I told her, "then doors will open." And they did. Before the week was out, two different groups called to ask me to speak to their leaders.

In most areas of my life at that time, I was very ambitious. This was different. This was God's personal invitation for me to work on his agenda, using the talents he'd given me, doing work that I sensed would be eternally significant. I felt grateful to be called to something important, but I wasn't thinking in terms of goals or timelines. I just wanted to be my best and do my best. I can honestly say that today, more than forty years later, I'm just as excited as I was that first day. I'm still thrilled to have been called to teach leadership and develop leaders. I want to add value to leaders who multiply value to others. That's my calling and purpose in life.

THE CHARACTERISTICS OF A CALLING

You have a purpose in life, too, and you can receive a sense of calling. I don't want you to miss this just because I'm telling you about my calling in the context of my faith. You can be of a different faith than me or have no faith at all, and you can still be called. Your calling can give you a fruitful and fulfilling life, one that fills you with passion and motivates you to make a difference. When it is your calling, you won't have to chase it. You will be *captivated* by it.

WHEN IT IS YOUR CALLING, YOU WON'T HAVE TO CHASE IT. YOU WILL BE *CAPTIVATED* BY IT.

I want to help you to understand calling so that you can find yours if you haven't already done so. I want you to be ready when it comes.

1. YOUR CALLING MATCHES WHO YOU ARE
No one has ever been called to do something he or she wasn't suited for. Calling always matches who you are. For that reason, it's important for you to be self-aware as you stay attentive to finding your calling.

CONSIDER

Here are some questions that can help you think about calling:

If you could do one thing for the rest of your life, even if you never got paid for it, what would you do?

_____

_____

_____

What experiences have you had that you desire to help others with?

_____

_____

_____

What do people often ask for your help with?

_____

_____

_____

What lights you up?

_____

_____

_____

What do you love learning about?

_____

_____

_____

What could you talk about for hours and hours?

_____

_____

_____

What activities are you always self-motivated to do?

_____

_____

_____

What can you do that makes a positive difference in the lives of others?

_____

_____

_____

What would you like to do that would live beyond you?

_____

_____

_____

The calling you receive often taps into not just one or two of these things but *all* of them. Look at your answers to those questions. What is the common thread?

_____

_____

_____

_____

_____

2. YOUR CALLING TAPS INTO YOUR PASSION

Impacting the world is hard. If you lack passion for the call, your energy will fizzle out. You should use the sleepless night test for this one. Is there a cause you want to pursue that is consuming you so much that you can't sleep at night? That's a sign that you might be called to it. I like the advice of author, philosopher, and civil rights leader Howard Thurman, who said, "Don't ask what the world needs. Ask what makes you come alive and go do it. Because what the world needs is people who have come alive." Passion is a great driver toward calling.

CONSIDER

What is your answer to Thurman's question? What makes you come alive?

_____

_____

_____

_____

_____

Talent, skills, experience, and opportunities all align with calling, but passion provides the fuel to pursue your calling.

3. YOUR CALLING IS IMPORTANT TO YOU, BUT IT'S NOT ABOUT YOU

A true calling is never about the person being called. It's about helping others. A calling moves us from the center of everything in our world to becoming the channel through which good things come to others. As Nelson Mandela said, "What counts in life is not the mere fact that we have lived. It is what difference we have made to the lives of others that will determine the significance of the life we lead." When you're called, you have an important role to play, but it's never about you.

CONSIDER

If you could do only one thing to help others in this world, what would it be?

_____

_____

_____

_____

4. YOUR CALLING IS BIGGER THAN YOU

A calling always involves something that feels big, something that's bigger than you are. It may intimidate you. It may even seem impossible. Yet you feel compelled to get out of your comfort zone to fulfill it. You are willing to stretch to complete it. You keep moving forward despite the odds.

5. YOUR CALLING CHANGES YOUR PERSPECTIVE

Having a calling makes you see your world differently. Where you once saw only obligations and responsibilities, you will begin to see options and opportunities. No longer will you be focused on the tasks you are required to do. A whole new world will open up to you of things you *want* to do.

CONSIDER

Take a look at the difference between the two perspectives of responsibility and opportunity. As you think about the one thing you might aspire to do in order to help others and improve the world, which phrase on each line best describes your perspective?

RESPONSIBILITY PERSPECTIVE	OPPORTUNITY PERSPECTIVE
❑ Feels Heavy	❑ Feels Light and Exciting
❑ Is a Burden	❑ Is a Privilege
❑ Consumes Energy	❑ Creates Energy
❑ Can Seem Meaningless and Rote	❑ Feels Purposeful and Meaningful
❑ Is Driven by a Sense of Duty	❑ Is Driven by a Sense of Optimism
❑ Is Something We Have to Do	❑ Is Something We Want to Do
❑ Leads to Routine and Repetition	❑ Inspires Creativity
❑ Discourages Efficiency	❑ Inspires Efficiency
❑ Tends to Drag Out Tasks	❑ Desires Bang for Our Buck
❑ Repels Others with Negativity	❑ Attracts Others with Positivity
❑ Gives a Sense of Completion	❑ Gives a Sense of Possibility
❑ Is Associated with Pushing	❑ Is Associated with Inspiring
❑ Leads to Success in 10 percent of Our Lives	❑ Leads to Success That Opens Up the Hidden 90 percent

A calling lifts our hearts and expands our options. It can make even the mundane meaningful. It drastically changes our perspective for the better.

6. YOUR CALLING GIVES YOU PURPOSE

Sheri Riley is a John Maxwell Team coach who has worked for many years with professional athletes and celebrity entertainers. She recently published her first book, called *Exponential Living*. In it she wrote about how many people get so caught up in the grind of life that they lose track of why they do it. She said:

> Many high achievers are so focused on working that work becomes an end in itself. They become addicted to the demands, the stress, and the sense of accomplishment they get from working hard, even if their hard work isn't leading them anywhere they want to go. Often, high achievers don't even realize they have achieved what they are working for and that it's time to move on to something else.
>
> Work is labor, folks. That's all it is. It has value only to the extent that it accomplishes something you truly desire. Many of us high achievers operate under some version of the Puritan work ethic. That is, we believe that work has value in and of itself. So therefore, if we do a lot of it, *we* must be valuable. So we take on lots of work, and keep ourselves very busy, but not necessarily as productive as we could. We exhaust ourselves because we confuse work with value. At the end of a tiring workweek, we look back and say, "Well, at least I did *that*." We may not be any closer to our dreams, but we sure did work.[3]

At one end of the spectrum are people like the ones Sheri described, the high achievers who work for the sake of work. On the other end are people who work because they have to but find no fulfillment in what they do. Author Seth Godin was talking to these people when he said, "Instead of wondering what your next vacation is, maybe you should set up a life you don't need to escape from." The answer for both types of people is the sense of purpose that comes with a calling.

7. YOUR CALLING HELPS YOU TO OVERCOME OBSTACLES

What do you draw upon when you hit a wall in your life or your leadership? Do you rely on grit? Do you draw upon discipline? Do you work harder? All of these things are good, but they can't compare to the power of calling to keep you going.

My friend Dave Ramsey said, "Higher calling matters. When you care so deeply about the why—why you're doing what you're doing—then and only then are you operating in a way that allows you to overcome the obstacles."

8. YOUR CALLING BRINGS FULFILLMENT

Nothing in life is as rewarding as fulfilling your calling—nothing. Wealth, fame, achievement, recognition: all of them fall short. Why do you think so many celebrities and athletes champion causes? They're looking for the fulfillment that comes only from pursuing a calling.

I've observed and known many who lived without a calling. As the years pass, their deepest needs and desires go unexplored. They are busy, but they develop a vague anxiety that their life has not achieved its ultimate meaning and significance. They live with a restlessness because they are not firmly attached to the moral purposes that give life its worth. Because they don't follow a calling, they lack the internal compass to make unshakable commitments. They never develop the inner consistency that they long for. Every day they come up short in obtaining the fulfillment they crave, and it frustrates them.

Calling changes everything. It's the missing piece in the puzzle. The plot in a good story. The musical note that completes the piece. Every day I experience the euphoric feeling of fulfillment as I write, speak, and lead. When I'm engaged in my calling, the sense that I experience is, "I was born for this!"

FINDING YOUR CALLING

So, what is your calling? Have you already discovered it? Are you finding clues as you answer the questions in this lesson? Or do you need some extra help finding your way? Fred Swaniker, the founder of the African Leadership Group, said, "Every now and then, we come to a fork in the road that requires us to either stay on our current life path, or change course and do something radically different." If you have not already found your calling, then you are at the fork in the road. I hope you will take the bold way, the radically different path that represents your calling. It may be frightening. It may be uncomfortable. It may feel uncertain. But I can assure you, if you find your calling, you will never regret the difficult journey taken to pursue it, because there's nothing else like it.

When I was in a class in college, a professor asked three questions to help us understand ourselves and find the pathway for our lives. Since I first heard them, I have asked them of myself repeatedly. Those three questions are:

1. What do I sing about? What fills my heart?
2. What do I cry about? What breaks my heart?
3. What do I dream about? What lifts my heart?

These questions set me on the journey that enabled me to discover my calling. As time went by, I experienced moments that spoke to me at a deep level of purpose:

- *Singing Moments*—Times when I knew that my leadership was making a positive difference for people.
- *Crying Moments*—Times when I wept because I saw that bad leadership misused or abused people.
- *Dreaming Moments*—Times when I dreamed of training leaders who would make a significant impact on people.

You'll notice that all these moments related to leadership because that's where my calling is.

CONSIDER

To find your calling, find what touches your heart. Answer the three questions:

What do you sing about? What fills your heart?

_____

_____

_____

_____

_____

_____

What do you cry about? What breaks your heart?

_____

_____

_____

What do you dream about? What lifts your heart?

_____

_____

_____

You may find your calling in a moment as I did, but I don't think you can force it to appear immediately if you haven't already discovered it. It usually takes time to unfold. I can look back at years of leadership moments, good and bad experiences, feelings of both discontent and contentment that set me up for my calling and prepared me for it. My best advice is to be attentive. Pay attention to your feelings. Take time to reflect. Learn from your experiences. Never dismiss your dreams. And when your moment comes, embrace it.

REVIEW AND RESPOND

Spend some time reviewing all of your responses in this lesson. Do you see a pattern that reveals or points in the direction of your calling? How do your answers line up? What is the common theme? What do you believe your purpose and calling might be? Describe it and date it here.

_____

_____

_____

_____

_____

_____

HOW TO MAXIMIZE YOUR CALLING

I don't know what phase of life you're in as you read this book. Maybe you're simply doing a job and hoping for more. Perhaps you've developed a career yet still long for something more. If either of these is true, keep working your way toward your calling. However, you might be in the season of life where you know your calling and you're working out what to do with it. If that describes you, then I want to give you some advice. And if this does not yet describe you, then mark these words for when you do enter your calling season:

1. INTEGRATE A DAILY FOCUS WITH A LONG-TERM PERSPECTIVE

In his book *The Life Cycle Completed*, Erik Erikson told a joke about a man who is on his deathbed. As he lay there with his eyes closed, his wife whispered to him, naming every member of the family who was there to wish him shalom. "And who," he suddenly asked, sitting up abruptly, "who is minding the store?"[4]

People who have a sense of calling need to maintain a daily focus without losing their long-term perspective. I think of this as using both the clock and the compass. The clock helps me to stay on track with what I'm doing today. It encourages me to invest in my daily activities and to keep appointments. It allows me to fulfill the mission of the moment.

The compass helps me to stay on track with my destiny. It allows me to focus on the vision. It helps me know where I'm going. I maintain my overall values. I keep the vision before me. It allows me to fulfill the mission of my calling.

CONSIDER

How can you use the idea of the clock and the compass to help keep you on track?

_____

_____

_____

_____

_____

2. SET A CLEAR PATH IN A WORTHWHILE DIRECTION

One of the paradoxes of life is that you must follow your calling with clarity and purpose while living with uncertainty. So go forward in a direction that is worthy of the expenditure of your life, and go with confidence, but expect to write your story in pencil—one that has an eraser! I say that because as you pursue your calling, your life will be written and rewritten. Some experiences will end in a period—a full stop. Others will need the pause of a comma. You will have exclamation mark moments of victory and contentment. And of course, there will be many question marks.

Where will you end up if you follow your calling? Only time will tell. But the journey will be worth it, and the story will be amazing.

3. ASK OTHERS TO JOIN WITH YOU AND YOUR CALLING

Because every person's true calling is bigger than the one who has been called, it always requires the aid of others to fulfill it. If you've found your calling and not yet asked others to join you in it, you have neglected a crucial step, and it's time to start enlisting help. People who are successful often leave an inheritance for others. People who fulfill a calling leave a legacy *in* others.

CONSIDER

Have you invited others to join you in the effort you are making to improve the world? If not, why not? Who can you invite now? If so, who are they, and are you doing all you can to empower and release them to make a difference?

_____

_____

_____

_____

_____

_____

_____

I hope you will do whatever you can to search for your calling, and then work with everything you have to fulfill it. And I hope that you will embrace not only this leadershift but all the other ones I've discussed in this book. Remember, every advance you make as a leader will require a leadershift that changes the way you think, act, and lead. You can only reach your potential if you embrace these leadershifts:

- Soloist to Conductor—The Focus Shift
- Goals to Growth—The Personal Development Shift
- Perks to Price—The Cost Shift
- Pleasing People to Challenging People—The Relational Shift
- Maintaining to Creating—The Abundance Shift
- Ladder Climbing to Ladder Building—The Reproduction Shift
- Directing to Connecting—The Communication Shift
- Team Uniformity to Team Diversity—The Improvement Shift
- Positional Authority to Moral Authority—The Influence Shift
- Trained Leaders to Transformational Leaders—The Impact Shift
- Career to Calling—The Passion Shift

Are there other leadershifts that you'll have an opportunity to make? Probably. I haven't yet discovered them, but if they're out there, I intend to. Why? Because long ago I made the personal development shift from goals to growth, and I'm still growing as a leader. If you're growing, you will discover them too. When you do, let me and others know about them. The better we can lead and help others to lead, the greater and more fulfilling our impact will be.

CAREER TO
CALLING

THE PASSION SHIFT

DISCUSSION QUESTIONS

1. Do you find it easy or difficult to believe that all people have a calling and can identify and embrace it if they're willing to try? Explain.

2. How would you describe your current work situation? You do a job, you are building a career, or you are fulfilling a calling. How content are you there?

3. How difficult do you think it is to find a purpose that makes the most of your talents, taps into your passion, fuels your passion, benefits others, is bigger than you, gives you purpose and perseverance, fulfills you, and draws you forward? Explain your answer.

4. How do you answer the questions about what makes you sing, cry, and dream?

5. Based upon what you know about yourself today, how would you describe your calling or purpose as you understand it so far? What action are you willing to take to pursue or fulfill it?

NOTES

ABOUT THE AUTHOR

John C. Maxwell is a #1 *New York Times* bestselling author, coach, and speaker who has sold more than 31 million books in fifty languages. He has been identified as the #1 leader in business by the American Management Association and the most influential leadership expert in the world by *Business Insider* and *Inc.* magazine. He is the founder of The John Maxwell Company, The John Maxwell Team, EQUIP, and the John Maxwell Leadership Foundation, organizations that have trained millions of leaders from every country of the world. A recipient of the Horatio Alger Award, as well as the Mother Teresa Prize for Global Peace and Leadership from the Luminary Leadership Network, Dr. Maxwell speaks each year to Fortune 500 companies, presidents of nations, and many of the world's top business leaders. He can be followed at Twitter.com/JohnCMaxwell. For more information about him visit JohnMaxwell.com.

ENDNOTES

Lesson One: Why Every Leader Needs to Leadershift

1. Eric J. McNulty, "Thinking Like a Leader: Three Big Shifts," Strategy and Business, July 28, 2015, https://www.strategy-business.com/blog/Thinking-Like-a-Leader-Three-Big-Shifts.
2. Bruna Martinuzzi, "The Agile Leader: Adaptability," Mindtools, accessed October 6, 2017, https://www.mindtools.com/pages/article/newLDR_49.htm.
3. *The Flux Report: Building a Resilient Workforce in the Face of Flux* (London: Right Management, 2014), p. 6, https://www.rightmanagement.co.uk/wps/wcm/connect/350a18c6-6b19-470d-adba-88c9e0394d0b/Right+Management+Flux+Report+Spread.pdf?MOD=AJPERES.
4. Paul Karofsky, quoted in Eric Yaverbaum, *Leadership Secrets of the World's Most Successful CEOs: 100 Top Executives Reveal the Management Strategies That Made Their Companies Great* (Chicago: Dearborn Trade, 2004), p. 161.
5. Maria Popova, "Malcolm Gladwell on Criticism, Tolerance, and Changing Your Mind," Brain Pickings, June 24, 2014, https://www.brainpickings.org/2014/06/24/malcolm-gladwell-nypl-interview/ (emphasis original).
6. C. Vijayakumar, "Three Key Steps to Making Sure Your Skills Stay Relevant," World Economic Forum, May 24, 2017, https://www.weforum.org/agenda/2017/05/3-key-steps-to-making-sure-your-skills-stay-relevant/.
7. Brad Lomenick, *The Catalyst Leader: 8 Essentials for Becoming a Change Maker* (Nashville: Thomas Nelson, 2013), pp. 111–112.

Lesson Two: Soloist to Conductor

1. Laurence Vittes, "Four Soloists Talk About Stepping Up to the Conductor's Podium," *Strings*, March 11, 2016, http://stringsmagazine.com/4-soloists-talk-about-stepping-up-to-the-conductors-podium/.
2. Matthew 25:40.
3. Matthew Kelly, *The Four Signs of a Dynamic Catholic: How Engaging 1% of Catholics Could Change the World* (Hebron, KY: Beacon Publishing, 2012), Kindle location 2382 of 2488.

Lesson Three: Goals to Growth

1. Adlai E. Stevenson, "The Educated Citizen," speech at Princeton University, March 22, 1954, transcript accessed January 10, 2018, http://infoshare1.princeton.edu/libraries/firestone/rbsc/mudd/online_ex/stevenson/adlai1954.html.
2. C. S. Lewis, *Of Other Worlds: Essays and Stories* (1966, New York: Houghton Mifflin Harcourt, 2002), p. 26.

Lesson Four: Perks to Price

1. Jim Collins, *Good to Great: Why Some Companies Make the Leap . . . and Others Don't* (New York: Harper Business, 2001), p. 85.
2. Ibid, p. 86.
3. Original source unknown.
4. Douglas L. Wilson and Rodney O. Davis, eds., *Herndon's Informants: Letters, Interviews, and Statements About Abraham Lincoln* (Champaign, IL: University of Illinois Press, 1998), p. 164.
5. "Cal Ripken's 2,131st Consecutive Game Is Major League Baseball's Most Memorable Moment," mlb.com, accessed December 11, 2017, http://www.mlb.com/mlb/events/memorable_moments/mlb-memorable_moments.jsp.
6. Bucky Fox, "Cal Ripken Wields an Iron Will While Winning in Baseball," *Investor's Business Daily*, August 26, 2017, https://www.investors.com/news/management/leaders-and-success/cal-ripken-wields-an-iron-will-while-winning-in-baseball/.

Lesson Five: Pleasing People to Challenging People

1. Seth Godin, *Poke the Box* (New York: Penguin, 2015), p. 25.

Lesson Six: Maintaining to Creating

1. Roger von Oech, *A Whack on the Side of the Head: How You Can Be More Creative*, 3rd ed. (New York: Warner Books, 1998).
2. Albert Einstein, quoted in Jeff Nilsson, "Albert Einstein: 'Imagination Is More Important Than Knowledge,'" *Saturday Evening Post*, March 20, 2010, http://www.saturdayeveningpost.com/2010/03/20/history/post-perspective/imagination-important-knowledge.html.
3. Thomas Edison, quoted in M. A. Rosanoff, "Edison in His Laboratory," *Harper's Magazine,* 135 (September 1932), p. 403, col. 2.
4. Hugh MacLeod, *Ignore Everybody: And 39 Other Keys to Creativity* (New York: Portfolio, 2009), p. 26.
5. As summarized in Martin Zwilling, "Follow Seven Rules for a Creative Startup Culture," *Forbes*, April 10, 2011, https://www.forbes.com/sites/martinzwilling/2011/04/10/follow-seven-rules-for-a-creative-startup-culture/.
6. Robert D. Kaplan, "Man Versus Afghanistan," *The Atlantic*, April 2010, https://www.theatlantic.com/magazine/archive/2010/04/man-versus-afghanistan/307983/.
7. Mary Ardito, "Creativity: It's the Thought That Counts," *Bell Telephone Magazine*, 61 (1), p. 33, https://quoteinvestigator.com/2014/03/03/creative-maya/.
8. Steve Pavlina, "Do It Now," StevePavlina.com (blog), November 28, 2005, https://www.stevepavlina.com/blog/2005/11/do-it-now/.
9. Warren Bennis, quoted in Max Cates, *Seven Steps to Success for Sales Managers: A Strategic Guide to Creating a Winning Sales Team Through Collaboration*, 1st ed. (Indianapolis: Pearson FT Press, 2015), p. 26.

Lesson Seven: Ladder Climbing to Ladder Building

1. Lead Through Strengths, "Explore the Clifton Strengthfinder Talent Theme—Woo," Strengthsfinder, accessed May 16, 2018, http://leadthroughstrengths.com/woo/.
2. Napoleon Hill, *The Law of Success* (New York: Penguin, 2008), p. 420.
3. Tim Elmore, "Becoming a Life Giving Mentor," October 19, 2012, *Growing Leaders: Ready for Real Life*, https://growingleaders.com/blog/life-giving-mentor/.

Lesson Eight: Directing to Connecting

1. Bob Buford, *Halftime: Moving From Success to Significance* (Grand Rapids: Zondervan, 2008), p. 118.
2. Stephen King, commencement address, Poughkeepsie, NY, Vassar College, May 20, 2001. Transcribed from "Vassar College Commencement," video, C-SPAN, May 20, 2001, https://www.c-span.org/video/?164360-1/vassar-college-commencement.
3. Mark Moring, "Chronicling Caspian," Christianity.com, May 1, 2008, https://www.christianity.com/11622775/.
4. Charles M. Schwab, "Mr. Carnegie Understood This Great Thing," *System* (June 1922), 679, accessed May 17, 2018, https://books.google.com/books?id=rQRKAQAAMAAJ&dq=System%20Charles%20Schwab%20exalted&pg=PA679.

Lesson Nine: Team Uniformity to Team Diversity

1. Jon R. Katzenbach and Douglas K. Smith, "The Discipline of Teams," *Harvard Business Review*, March–April 1993, https://hbr.org/1993/03/the-discipline-of-teams-2.
2. Patrick Lencioni, *The Five Dysfunctions of a Team: A Leadership Fable* (San Francisco: Josey-Bass, 2002), p. 202.
3. Ibid, pp. 202–203.
4. Christie Smith and Stephanie Turner, *The Radical Transformation of Diversity and Inclusion: The Millennial Influence* (Westlake, TX: Deloitte University, 2015), p. 7, https://www2.deloitte.com/content/dam/Deloitte/us/Documents/about-deloitte/us-inclus-millennial-influence-120215.pdf.
5. Ibid., p. 5.
6. Ibid., p. 11.
7. Ibid., p. 13.

8. Tomas Chamorro-Premuzic, "Does Diversity Actually Increase Creativity?" *Harvard Business Review*, June 28, 2017, https://hbr.org/2017/06/does-diversity-actually-increase-creativity.

9. Stefanie K. Johnson, "What 11 CEOs Have Learned About Championing Diversity," *Harvard Business Review*, updated August 29, 2017, https://hbr.org/2017/08/what-11-ceos-have-learned-about-championing-diversity.

10. 1Chamorro-Premuzic, "Does Diversity Actually Increase Creativity?"

Lesson Ten: Positional Authority to Moral Authority

1. Kevin Sharer, "How Moral Authority Manifests in Truly Impactful Leaders," *The Harbus*, March 17, 2017, http://www.beatthegmat.com/mba/2017/03/17/moral-authority-in-truly-impactful-leader.

2. Chuck Olson, "Four Ways to Build Moral Authority," Lead with Your Life (website), January 5, 2016, https://leadwithyourlife.com/4-ways-to-build-moral-authority/.

3. George Lewis Davis, *Magic Shortcuts to Executive Success: 37 Ways and Timely Moves That Can Smooth the Path and Lead to More Rapid Promotion and More Important Jobs* (Upper Saddle River, NJ: Prentice Hall, 1962), p. 110.

4. Doug Hall with David Wecker, *Making the Courage Connection: How People Get from Fear to Freedom—and How You Can Too* (New York: Fireside, 1997), p. 47.

5. Andy Stanley, *Visioneering: God's Blueprint for Developing and Maintaining Vision* (Colorado Springs: Multnomah, 1999), p. 179.

Lesson Eleven: Trained Leaders to Transformational Leaders

1. Lawrence Tribble, "Awaken" (c. 1780), Push Back Now (website), October 31, 2011, http://pushbacknow.org/2011/10/31/awaken-a-1700s-poem-by-lawrence-tribble/comment-page-1/.

2. Walter E. Fauntroy, quoted in Pat Williams with Jim Denney, *The Pursuit: Wisdom for the Adventure of Your Life* (Ventura, CA: Regal, 2008), p. 196.

Lesson Twelve: Career to Calling

1. Amy Wrzesniewski et al., "Jobs, Careers, and Callings: People's Relations to Their Work," *Journal of Research in Personality* 31 (1997), pp. 21–33, http://faculty.som.yale.edu/amywrzesniewski/documents/Jobscareersandcallings.pdf.

2. Richard Leider, "Is Leading Your Calling?" *Leader to Leader*, Winter 2004, http://www.geneva.edu/graduate/assets/msol_writing_sample_article.pdf, p. 2.

3. Sheri Riley, *Exponential Living: Stop Spending 100% of Your Time on 10% of Who You Are* (New York: New American Library, 2017), p. 191.

4. Erik Erikson, quoted in Emily Esfahani Smith, "Psychology Shows It's a Big Mistake to Base Our Self-Worth on Our Professional Achievements," Quartz, May 24, 2017, https://qz.com/990163/psychology-shows-its-a-big-mistake-to-base-our-self-worth-on-our-professional-achievements/.

LEADERSHIP
FOUNDATION

transforming
LEADERS

transforming
COUNTRIES

Together,
WE CAN CHANGE THE WORLD.
jmlf.org

THE JOHN MAXWELL LEADERSHIP BLOG

Every week John Maxwell and CEO of The John Maxwell Enterprise, Mark Cole, share their in-the-moment thoughts on leadership and how to navigate your personal growth journey week by week.

LEADERSHIP IS TAUGHT.
DEVELOP THE LEADERS WITHIN
YOUR COMPANY.

When you begin to invest in your human capital, watch what happens. Your workforce becomes aligned with your corporate initiatives. They begin supporting critical business priorities and change efforts, AND your business success begins to accelerate.

LEADERSHIP DEVELOPMENT   **EMPLOYEE ENGAGEMENT**   **CHANGE MANAGEMENT**

DOWNLOAD OUR FREE DIGITAL RESOURCE!

Thinking Like A Leader: The Top Ten Truths about Leading

johnmaxwellcompany.com/leadership

The JOHN MAXWELL **Co.**
CORPORATE LEADERSHIP SOLUTIONS

To learn more about our corporate training programs, contact our Corporate Leadership Solutions Division.

johnmaxwellcompany.com

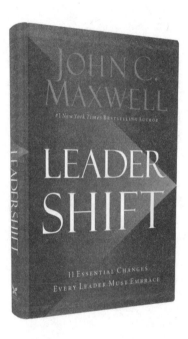